*Thank you  
For your love & support!  
God Bless your family*

Good Things Are Supposed To Happen To YOU!

# Good Things
## Are Supposed To Happen
## To
# YOU!

*"For I know the plans I have for you," declares the Lord. "Plans to prosper you and not to harm you. Plans to give you hope and an expected end." —Jeremiah 29:11*

Plus 7 Steps to Achieve Any Goal!

## Joey Noone

XULON PRESS

Xulon Press
2301 Lucien Way #415
Maitland, FL 32751
407.339.4217
www.xulonpress.com

© 2019 by Joey Noone

All rights reserved solely by the author. The author guarantees all contents are original and do not infringe upon the legal rights of any other person or work. No part of this book may be reproduced in any form without the permission of the author. The views expressed in this book are not necessarily those of the publisher.

Scripture quotations taken from the Holy Bible, New International Version (NIV). Copyright © 1973, 1978, 1984, 2011 by Biblica, Inc.™. Used by permission. All rights reserved.

Printed in the United States of America.

ISBN-13: 9781545671665

# *Joey Noone*

Who is Joey Noone?

Joey Noone—affectionately known as Joey Voices—is a professional singing comedian and impressionist turned speaker and author with his first book, *Good Things Are Supposed to Happen to YOU*.

Born Joseph Paul Noone in Melrose, Massachusetts (his mom's hometown), in 1972, Joey was raised one city away, in his dad's hometown of Malden, Massachusetts. Malden was the first town to enter the American Revolution—a historical fact Joey is quite proud of.

Joey is a seven-year theological seminary graduate, having earned bachelor's and master's degrees in systematic theology from ACTS Theological Seminary, in Plymouth, Massachusetts. Joey is a prolific songwriter as well, with country songs like "Do It All Again," "Important Things," and "Sweet Tori," to name a few.

Joey is the youngest and most energetic of eight kids (four boys, four girls) in a big Irish family. He has been a regular on AM 680 WRKO Boston Talk Radio since 2005 and is currently promoting his Las Vegas–style stage-show with the *Wicked Bites* Radio/TV program in Boston, Massachusetts (formerly the *Pat Whitley Restaurant Show*).

Joey also had a brief stint with *The Joey Voices Radio Show* in 2015 on AM 1510 WMEX Boston Talk Radio before moving on from that to pursue bigger endeavors.

# *Foreword*

*I* met Joey Noone a few years ago at the Italian American Sports Hall of Fame banquet in Malden, Massachusetts. We talked about a variety of things: his very funny and entertaining Las Vegas style stage show - JOEY VOICES, comprised of comedy singing impersonations of numerous celebrity voices. We also talked about the Red Sox, Patriots, Celtics and Bruins, and how life has been very good to both of us.

Somehow, we got onto the subject of faith and realized that we had quite a bit in common. Joey mentioned that his Christian faith changed his life completely and I told him how it also changed mine many years ago, when our family needed the Lord to get us through a very tough physical and emotional time in our lives.

This book can change your life. The chapters about transforming our minds and truly believing that we can achieve our dreams and fulfill our needs applies to every one of us.

Joey uses himself as an example of how his commitment to Jesus Christ as his Lord and Savior through Scripture got him on the correct path in his life. If you are living in darkness and need the true light of life this book is a Godsend.

Joey Voices is his stage name, but it is very appropriate that he is recognized with that name in this book as well, because Joey Noone is the "voice" of his Christian faith when it comes down to getting the word of the Lord out. I am honored to help share this WORD.

Rico Petrocelli
Boston Red Sox Hall of Famer (1963, 65-76)

# *Introduction*

*I*magine if it was possible for you to take back your happiness? Imagine if you could learn how to think better than you do right now? Is your walk with God suffering because of your own faulty thinking about yourself and life in general? Have you been seeking a more fruitful relationship with Him? Or how about more fruitful relationships with the people in your life? This book will show you how to accomplish these things and more!

*Good Things Are Supposed to Happen to YOU* is not a book of stories about good things happening to people. Rather it's a book about how to reprogram the subconscious mind in order to take back your happiness and the control of your conscious, thinking mind so that good things can and will happen to you. This will create a vibrant, invigorating and more fulfilling life experience. Just as different body parts make up a complete human body, *Good Things Are Supposed to Happen to YOU* comprises many different principles for that common goal.

This book will inform you about a lot of things throughout as you will see, including:

- How to reprogram your mind.
- You exist for good things to happen to you, but trials will inevitably also happen in order that the resistance thereof may build your spiritual muscles—if you let it.
- The law of attraction—what it is and what it is *not*.
- Where you stand with God, and does He love *you*?
- The blessings of living by biblical principles.
- God's dynamic power.
- Man's power to create either misery or blessings in his life by how he views humanity, the world, and his place/purpose in the world.
- How your mental paradigm (thought pattern) shapes your world from the inside out.
- Your consistent thought patterns eventually develop into tangible things in your life.
- The subconscious mind is the connecting link between the finite mind of man and infinite mind of God.
- Imagination is the preview of your life.
- The power of specific intention
- The power of suggestion

- The transforming power of gratitude.
- Reaping what you sow.
- The Gospel of Jesus Christ. What it is and what it means to your eternal destiny.

All these principles are the topics of great conversation that, if applied to your life, will bring about the good things that are supposed to happen to you.

*Good Things Are Supposed to Happen to YOU* is the juxtaposition to the negative twenty-four-hour news media. Every day, negative news constantly plants the subliminal message into the subconscious mind of the average citizen that bad things are supposed to happen to them, because it's mostly what they see when they turn on the news.

One of the things I wish to accomplish with this book is to show Christians that they can be happy, more fruitful and blessed in their walk with Christ. That good things are supposed to happen to them, hence the reason we live in these physical bodies equipped with the five tactile senses. This book also focuses on what the law of attraction is and more importantly, what it is not and how to take back control of your thinking mind per mental re-programming techniques—to think only on the good that you want in order to bring more of it into your life. As you focus on what you want your subconscious mind filters out what you don't want. This book will help you learn how to re-program your subconscious mind.

I also wrote this book for the people who may choose a path other than Christianity. I hope and pray they do not, as I can testify that living in Christ is truly living with an eternal purpose. I'll show them that even though according to the Word of God there is no salvation apart from the blood of Jesus (Jn 14:6, Acts 2:38–41, Heb 9:22), if they will at least utilize the principles described in this book and again, take back control of their thinking mind, they can be positive, fruitful, productive people in society according to the law of reciprocity (sowing and reaping) and sympathetic resonance (I'll define the latter as we move along in the chapter).

You all know what the law of sowing and reaping is, but you may not be familiar with the law of sympathetic resonance. Did you know you can change your circumstances from bad to good simply by consciously changing the way you feel inside and then holding onto that feeling? The stronger the feeling, the quicker the change in your circumstances.

Now, I'm not saying things will magically change instantly to your naked eye, but reality will have to correspond to how you're feeling by meeting that positive, consistent energy with like positive energy. You immediately start the process of positive change in your circumstances by changing the way you consistently think, which changes the way you feel inside.

Life responds to what you want either positively or negatively, but there's a difference between wanting something and needing it. Did you ever notice how when you want something it's a positively confident feeling inside to the point of almost knowing it will be yours one fine day?

Now, contrast that with the spirit of needing that very same thing. It's a feeling of desperation that repels that which you are needing. Whenever you feel desperate about anything put it down and walk away from it, no matter how hard it is to do. For you now know that it will never be yours so long as you're in the spirit of needing it.

Here is the law of sympathetic resonance. Think of two pianos in one room. You strike the C note on one piano and the C on the other piano begins to vibrate with sympathetic resonance in response to the stimulation of the sound vibration.

Well, human beings put out certain vibrations—both emotional and sound, either positive or negative. Anyone within range of each other, like the two pianos, will pick up a vibe and resonate with it if they are vibrating on that same thought/feeling frequency. As you read this book, please remember that everything is vibrational energy that operates by the law of cause and effect, which states that you can cause an effect with your thoughts, feelings, words and actions.

It is my hope and prayer that this book is a rich blessing to you. I also hope you grow into someone better, smarter and even more loving than you were before reading it.

I want *Good Things Are Supposed to Happen to YOU* to shine a light on the object of the human brain from a different angle. To change the understanding of who man is as compared to all Creation and to God. Man possesses the ability to think multiple levels deep. In other words, man can think about thinking, and then think about thinking about thinking, and so on and so forth. Man can also go on to explain this concept in a very cogent way. No other species has this awareness of conscious ability. This is what the Bible means when it says man was created in the image of God.

I believe man is also created physically in the image of God, and Jesus was the supreme example of this. "The Son is the radiance of God's glory and the exact representation of his being, sustaining all things by his powerful word. After he had provided purification for sins, he sat down at the right hand of the Majesty in heaven; So, he became as much superior to the angels as the name he has inherited is superior to theirs" (Heb 1:3–4).

Because man possesses the ability to consciously think, he also owns the ability to imagine his life — to plan it out and act, hopefully according to God's perfect will for him, as He (God) guides him. When man reprograms his mind with daily positive personal affirmations, those affirmations literally manifest his physical world around him, as his decision-making process becomes more positive. When Jesus encountered the blind men in Matthew 9:29–30, " Then he touched their eyes and said, "According to your faith let it be done to you"; and their sight was restored."

As a man's faith believes, it will be done unto him. Reprogramming your mind is not as hard as you think, but just like getting good at playing shortstop, you need to catch ground balls over and over until it becomes second nature to you.

When it becomes part of your autonomic system, you will know that your mind has been reprogrammed as your results begin to change. It takes dedication! The question is how bad do you want it?

Lastly, *Good Things Are Supposed to Happen to YOU* will assist you in doing your part at adding value to the world, making it a better and happier place to live. Thank you and happy reading!

# *Dedication*

This book is dedicated to three people. The first person is Jesus Christ, for teaching me His Holy Word in theological seminary and utilizing Rev. Dr. Joel F. Botelho, senior pastor of Temple Christ Messiah in Plymouth, Massachusetts, as the instrument to help me learn and remember my course of studies. Jesus Christ has given me the cerebral ability to spiritually understand and pay that truth forward through the echo chambers of this book.

Thank You, Father God!

The second person is my dad, attorney Thomas P. Noone. Dad raised me with honor and principles and always believed in me when I was an impetuous, rebellious teenager getting into fights just about every week, or so it seems in retrospect. It was my dad who loved me so much and never gave up on me. I became the man I am today because of this good man's great love.

Thank you, daddy-o! I love and miss you every single day!

The third person is my mom, Dorothy M. Noone. Mom has always seen me as her baby, even till the day she went home to be with The Lord. She would often remind me of all the times she took me on the bus to the square and walked around with me everywhere when I was a little boy.

Mom would always tell me how important a man my daddy was and would even take me down to city hall to visit him and Malden Mayor Jim Conway in their offices on occasion. Dad was the city solicitor in the Conway administration in the mid-late 1970s.

I told my mama I was going to write this book to help her reprogram her mind to be even more positive in life. This reprogramming would have enabled her to adopt a winning attitude in all circumstances of life, but she passed away on February 15, 2019 at age 80 before its release.

Mom is the reason I tried to fast track this book.

I *love* you, Mama, with all my heart! Rest-In-Peace eternally in the loving arms of Christ Jesus.

DEDICATION

## *Table of Contents*

Chapter 1: Good Things Are Supposed to
    Happen to Me . . . . . . . . . . . . . . . . . . . . . . . 1
Chapter 2: The Salvation of David Noone . . . . . . . . . . 4
Chapter 3: Michael . . . . . . . . . . . . . . . . . . . . . . . . . . . . 8
Chapter 4: Flutie Physics . . . . . . . . . . . . . . . . . . . . . . . 12
Chapter 5: Intention . . . . . . . . . . . . . . . . . . . . . . . . . . . 16
Chapter 6: Coming Attractions . . . . . . . . . . . . . . . . . . 34
Chapter 7: You Were Once Dead . . . . . . . . . . . . . . . . 41
Chapter 8: Reprogram Your Mind . . . . . . . . . . . . . . . 44
Chapter 9: A Grateful Heart . . . . . . . . . . . . . . . . . . . . 47
Chapter 10: Mental Pharmacy . . . . . . . . . . . . . . . . . . . 52
Chapter 11: From the Inside Out . . . . . . . . . . . . . . . . 56
Chapter 12: Always Smile . . . . . . . . . . . . . . . . . . . . . . 61
Chapter 13: Manifold Manifest. . . . . . . . . . . . . . . . . . 64
Chapter 14: The Law of Giving and Receiving . . . . . 67
Chapter 15: Always Say Yes. . . . . . . . . . . . . . . . . . . . . 70
Chapter 16: One, Two, Three Punch. . . . . . . . . . . . . . 73

Chapter 17: Hitler Got away with It . . . . . . . . . . . . . . 78
Chapter 18: Revisiting Paradigms . . . . . . . . . . . . . . 84
Chapter 19: The Dunamis of God. . . . . . . . . . . . . . . 89
Chapter 20: Never Stop Asking What If. . . . . . . . . . 93
Epilogue . . . . . . . . . . . . . . . . . . . . . . . . . . . . . . . . . . 99
Supplement: Seven Steps to Achieve any Goal . . . . 105
Acknowledgements. . . . . . . . . . . . . . . . . . . . . . . . . 113
Reviews. . . . . . . . . . . . . . . . . . . . . . . . . . . . . . . . . . 115

## Chapter 1

# *Good Things Are Supposed to Happen to Me*

———•———

*I could have been born an ant, but I wasn't. I could have been born a bear, a penguin or a giraffe, but I wasn't....I was born a human being, with an intellect and a conscience unlike any other species on the planet.*

One day I was listening to a motivational preacher named Les Brown, and he said something that instantly filled my heart with great hope and power. He said, "Now, I want you to repeat after me: Good things are supposed to happen to me!"

When I heard those words I immediately thought, "Yes! Good things are supposed to happen to me. I believe that!"

That was a powerful moment in my life at age forty-four. I'd been researching quantum entanglement, the law of attraction, and the law of giving and receiving for about eight months at that time. It was that one simple statement said so powerfully that got me to question why I should ever feel like I'm not worthy of God's very best in my life. I mean, after all He did create me, right?

Then one day about four months later, the idea hit me to write a book with God's Scriptures about how He loves us—how, like any good father, He wants to give good things to his children. To simplify, God wants to give good things to His kids and have good things happen to them in this life according to His good purpose. As Jesus said in

John 10:10b; "I have come that they might have life and that they might have it to the full" (KJV says "more abundantly").

Now, this does not mean there will not be hardships allowed by God due to the curse of sin upon mankind and the earth, as a result of the fall of man in Eden (Gen 3). This truly tests and strengthens our faith because let's face it, you can't have a testimony without a few tests.

I understood afterward that I was born to be great and to do great things. I finally believed that wholeheartedly without question. I mean, I could have been born an ant, but I wasn't. I could have been born a bear, a penguin or a giraffe (Hello up there!), but I wasn't. I could have been born a cat or a dog (and I like most dogs more than I do some people), but I wasn't.

I was born a human being, with an intellect and a conscience unlike any other species on the planet. We are all created in the image of Almighty God. I was born to achieve greatness—to do great things in life for the benefit of my fellow man.

Hence, I was now further encouraged and inspired to believe in that purpose.

*BELIEVE GOOD THINGS ARE SUPPOSED TO HAPPEN AND THEY WILL!*

## Chapter 2

# *The Salvation of David Noone*

---

*At least 250 pastors leave their ministries each month due to burnout, conflict, or moral failure. This is astounding.*

*E*ncouragement is the simplest thing in the world. It helps people to believe in themselves. You just need to explain and word it in a way they've never heard before, so that it breaks upon the heart of their understanding. It's funny how one cleverly worded phrase or coincidental moment can so profoundly change a person's entire outlook on life. So much that it changes them forever. I was present for a few such moments. However, one moment in-particular hits home and stands out vividly.

One night about 13 years ago my brother David was in my truck with me and I was dropping him off. I refused to let him out until he listened to a sermon written by a fellow Christian named Bill Wiese. Bill has become a friend of mine since interviewing him on my radio show here in Boston about his personal story and testimony for Jesus Christ.

Bill wrote the number one New York Times bestseller *23 Minutes in Hell*. It's about a vision the Lord gave him one night at 3:00 in the morning. The book describes Bill Wiese's out-of-body experience in Hell. It was neither a dream nor a near-death experience, but a vision as described in 2 Corinthians 12:1–2.

If you haven't read his book, please do so. It's the most amazing story I've ever heard in my life. In fact, I asked Bill Wiese on my Boston talk radio show about people who challenged his story. Asking whether he was being truthful about it or not because of how unbelievable a story it is.

It was a great interview to say the least and I personally believe him, as he stood nothing to gain by lying. He could have simply written it as a work of fiction with the Scriptures to back up the story and it would have been a bestseller anyway! Bill Wiese travels worldwide giving his testimony and doesn't take any speaking fees.

In the sermon at one point, Bill Wiese said The Lord had sent him to hell in his vision as an unsaved soul. He spoke of a giant demon that was torturing him and described this demon in specific detail. I looked at my brother, who was listening intently. His face turned white. I immediately paused the CD and asked what was wrong. David replied with eyes wide open, "This guy just described the demon I saw drawn on the wall of my jail cell last month. I'll never forget that thing for as long as I live because I had nothing but time to closely inspect how it was drawn. The guy who drew it had to have been demon possessed because the guy on that CD just described it to a T!"

Now, I could never have foreseen the transformation that was about to happen to my brother, David over the next six months. He got saved, became a Born Again, Christian (as Jesus describes in John 3:3-7), started his studies at ACTS Theological Seminary with me that fall and graduated after eight years with his doctorate in systematic theology. He is now an ordained minister. I finished seven years in 2014, earning my Master of Theology degree.

I invited my brother on the show to talk with Bill Wiese, but he politely declined, as he is not the limelight type. He was born to preach the Good Word, I was born to entertain and spread the Good Word in a different way. He wished me blessings and congratulated me on landing the interview. When I interviewed Bill Wiese about his book and told him my brother's story in greater detail, I told him that his testimony had saved David's life and added not only another soul to the Kingdom of Heaven, but another preacher to the battle for the souls of men.

Preaching seems to be a dying profession. I didn't realize this until I conducted my own research and discovered one source—Mark Dance, of lifeway.com. Dance wrote in September 2016 that at least 250 pastors leave their ministries each month due to burnout, conflict, or moral failure. This is astounding.

After telling Bill of how his story saved my brother's life, he humbly said to me, "Joey, it's an honor to be on your radio show and to have been a part of your brother's salvation, but as you know, the glory goes to Jesus. I take no credit as I'm just an instrument of God." What a humble man.

I said, "Amen to that, brother! Thank you for being an honored guest on my radio show, and God bless your family."

## Chapter 3

## *Michael*

---

*He (God) works miracles through our faith
in His love and abilities.*

*I* never understood how the human mind operated scientifically until I began learning about Quantum Entanglement (I'll define that in Chapter 5), the law of intention, and the power of suggestion. This is when I looked back on all the seeming coincidences of talking or having dreams about people I hadn't seen or heard from in a while and then suddenly showing up or calling me right after that. It all suddenly began to make sense to me.

One afternoon back in 2003, I was taking a nap and had a dream about a kid named Michael, whom I hadn't seen since the Glenwood Elementary School in Malden,

Massachusetts. I used to pick on Michael twenty-two years earlier.

I woke up from the dream weeping over how I'd treated him when we were little kids. While I was driving my mom to Walgreens, I was telling her the story, still weeping over how badly I felt about it. Well, as we were walking into Walgreens I literally bumped into a guy in the doorway as he was coming out. I said, "Excuse me, I'm so sorry!" I realized it was Michael from elementary school. I said, "Michael?"

He said, "Joey?"

We asked each other how life was for a moment and then I turned to my mom and said, "Ma, this is Michael, whom I was just telling you about in the car."

Mom's face turned every shade of pale as she looked up at him and then at me, with her mouth wide open. She said hello to him, and I said, with tears in my eyes, "Mike, I'm so sorry about how I treated you when we were young. Please forgive me."

He grabbed me by my shoulder, looked me in the eyes and said, "Joey, it's ok! We were kids, and it was a long time ago."

I told him I was a Christian and how God had fully softened my heart through His Word and Holy Spirit (though I'm still a work in progress to this day). I told him he looked great, and he did. He looked like a handsome Hollywood movie star—Hollywood hair and all.

I then wished him a happy Thanksgiving and went into the store with my mom. I was completely blown away at how I'd dreamt about him not fifteen minutes earlier and then voila, there he was right in front of me after twenty-two years!

Now, I believe God allowed me to have that dream, knowing I would bump into Michael right after that. However, after learning about quantum entanglement, I can see scientifically how my subconscious mind could have intelligently picked up on the vibrational wavelength of Michael if perhaps he was thinking about me, the very moment I was dreaming about him that afternoon. That subatomic thought wave signal was instantly sent to my subconscious mind (or more apropos, awakened), connecting us by an invisible field of information, delivering his memory to me in my dream and maybe that's how God used the science thereof to divinely appoint the two of us to meet at that moment in space/time at Walgreens to make amends.

The science of quantum physics seems to explain what always seemed supernatural to me and still is compared to my own natural ability. God created science and the discovery of quantum mechanics to show us just how prayer works and how powerful God is in our lives. Not only that, but it shows how He works miracles through our faith in His love and abilities. Our belief in our prayers for what we need and want can literally manifest those things through channels only God can foresee, like the right people coming into our lives to help facilitate our career/mission and the divine direction of our lives according to His plan.

Science is not anti-God nor vice versa. If it were then it would not make sense that new scientific discoveries would point *to* Him and not away from Him. Biochemistry shows us how quantum physics gave us wireless connection and the internet. Nikola Tesla was truly a mind ahead of his time.

# Chapter 4

## *Flutie Physics*

———•———

*God operates through science to interact with mankind….All intelligent information makes its way to its intended target*

About ten years ago, circa 2007, I was sitting in my office one evening and football legend Doug Flutie's name popped into my head out of nowhere, after I hadn't heard his name or seen him in the news for a long time.

A minute later my phone rang, and I answered, "Hello, Joey Voices."

On the other end was a gentleman who said he was from a certain Autism organization. I said, "Let me guess, you're with Doug Flutie?"

He said, "Yes, how did you know?"

I said, "Lucky guess."

# Flutie Physics

He said he was working with Flutie on a fundraiser for autism and asked if I would donate tickets to one of my upcoming shows for them to raffle off.

I said, "Give me your address and I'll mail you out two pair."

Now, that may sound creepy, but I was astounded that it happened to me. It opened my mind to the fact that God operates through science to interact with mankind. I figured it had something to do with intelligent information leaving the human mind and traveling somehow over the electrically charged airwave molecules of the atmosphere to the intended person on the other end. Mind you, I hadn't yet learned what quantum theory was, but as it turns out I was right!

All intelligent information makes its way to its intended target, which explains why Doug Flutie's name reached me a minute before my phone rang.

The same thing happened to me a few months later when I was performing for the Lawrence Eagle Tribune newspaper in North Andover, Massachusetts. I was wrapping up my chords and across the room I saw a guy I'd never seen before make eye contact with me from about twenty feet away. Just then the name "Feast of the Three Saints" popped into my head.

The gentleman picked up his folder off the table and made a beeline for me. He introduced himself and asked, "Are you available Labor Day weekend?"

I said, "Let me guess, feast of the three saints?"

He looked stunned as he shook my hand and said, "Yes! How did you know that?"

I laughed and said, "Lucky guess. Here's my card, give me a call."

I didn't dare tell him that I basically, albeit unintentionally, read his mind. He would have thought I was a cuckoo and I didn't even know how it happened scientifically at that time so I couldn't explain it to him, nor would I have even had the time.

In a similar occurrence last year, I was with a friend I hadn't seen in several years. He mentioned a girl named Ursula whom we both grew up with in Malden, Massachusetts. Now, Ursula is a unique name and I only knew one other Ursula, whom I met when I moved down to the south shore of Boston to Marshfield, Massachusetts. I moved there to finish my theological studies at ACTS Theological Seminary in Plymouth, Massachusetts.

I met Ursula while living in Marshfield, and she became one of my closest friends. In 2015, a year after I'd graduated, I moved back home to the north shore to my hometown of Malden, Massachusetts (the first town to enter the American Revolution on April 19, 1775). Ursula and I did not talk for a while after this life event.

Well, as I was talking with my friend about the Ursula we grew up with, I started to tell him about my Marshfield friend Ursula, and within about two minutes my phone rang. It was Marshfield Ursula calling me.

It was too loud to answer so I let it go to voicemail. This is the voicemail she left me: "Hey, buddy, I was just thinking about you. Haven't talked to you in quite a while and wanted to check in to see how you're doing. Give me a call."

Now, I'd just started researching the physics of quantum entanglement, so I immediately knew that my mention of her had instantaneously reached her subconscious. My name popped into her mind and she called me. I know it seems phenomenal that something freaky like that could even happen, but again, it's called quantum entanglement, which I will define in Chapter 5. Again, wireless connection was invented as a result of quantum physics. It has proven that things like this happen more often than we realize.

Had I not begun researching quantum physics I would have simply chalked it up to coincidence and said to her, "Wow! Your ears must have been ringing. I was just talking about you." However, by that time I had a basic understanding of how thought waves work on a subatomic level. I must admit it has been a few years since I began researching QP and I haven't been this on fire about a subject since I began learning about the Word of God (the Holy Bible).

## Chapter 5

# *Intention*

---

*Man has a powerful intent just by thinking sincerely about others and even about his own future goals.*

Intention simply put means, willing one's intention upon another person, thing, or circumstance, ergo when a person wants a job so badly, they simply won't take "NO" for an answer. They keep showing up at the job site until the boss finally hires them, just so the person will stop bothering him. I also call that "Polite Persistence," which is an extremely powerful tool in your victory toolbox. There are more examples of this, and I'll share a few with you to help you see the power you have within yourself. You will attain in life what you specifically intend with great passion, consistency, and determination—so long as God allows it as part of His plan for your life as He is in sovereign control over all Creation, with the exception of man's free will to come to the Cross of Salvation – Mk 16:16; Acts 2:38.

In the late 1960s, there was a fellow named Cleve Backster who was a CIA master interrogator. He also studied bio-communications. While in his lab one day, he wanted to experiment with a plant to see if it was aware of other life forms around it. He proceeded to hook up the leads from his polygraph machine to the Dracaena cane plant in his lab, and then turned on the machine.

Cleve experimented by dipping one of the leaves in coffee to see if it would react on the polygraph read, but nothing happened. He then thought to set the plant on fire. Immediately the needle spiked to the top of the graph. Cleve got up, walked over to his desk to retrieve a book of matches out of the desk drawer and as he walked back over to the plant, the needle was still pinned to the top of the graph. Cleve then changed his mind about burning the plant and returned the matches to the desk drawer. The needle suddenly dropped and went down back to normal. The plant was apparently frightened of the harm he intended to inflict upon it and responded dramatically.

Cleve then tried to reenact the experiment and pretended that he wanted to burn the plant again, but because his intent was contrived, the plant did not respond. Cleve never said he was going to set the plant on fire, he only thought it, but the plant read and felt his intention energetically with an instinctive consciousness that can't be explained in terms of human consciousness, as plants have no brains, only instinct. This implies that consciousness somehow on some level transcends grey matter and that humans are so much more than the physical bodies we walk around in.

Now, I'm not saying that plants have an intelligent consciousness like humans created in God's image. However, I am saying that all life responds to intent to harm and to love, especially human intent. The consciousness of that Dracaena cane plant on a subatomic cellular level, is no less than quantum entanglement as you will see.

Cleve went so far as to leave the lab and go miles away and he documented whenever he had a moment where he killed a bug, cooked anything with micro-bacteria, etc. The Dracaena plant spiked on the graph every time. Coincidence? Cleve Backster devoted the rest of his life to bio-communications, and you can read all his findings in his book *Primary Perception*.

Cleve Backster's experiment with the Dracaena plant shows us that if a plant can sense whether human intention is genuine or contrived, then how much more can another human?

One of the more popular experiments on the power of intention is human intent on water, in another experiment performed by Dr. Masaru Emoto and described in his book *The Hidden Messages in Water*, published in July 2011.

He took two clean glasses of water and taped words to each one. The first glass had harmful words, like, "I hate you," "I'm going to kill you," and "I hope you die" etc. written on it. The other glass had healing words like "I love you," "You're beautiful," and "Thank you" written on it. He had two groups of people think both sets of words with conviction as they directed their intent toward both glasses of water. The findings were astonishing.

Both glasses of water were put under a microscope after a time period and the glass with the healing words showed pure snowflake type crystals, while the glass with the harmful words showed murky decaying mold. This experiment has been conducted many times with the same results.

Now, the human body is more than two thirds water. If people can merely think evil and loving thoughts toward a glass of water and affect it in such a profound way, then how much more can we affect others we may hate or love? Especially ourselves! This makes you kind of want to apologize to yourself for self-deprecating thoughts and allowing people into your life who mistreat you. Time to clean house, eh? The good news is you can repair your water by changing the way you think about yourself and life in general.

Quantum entanglement, with regards to intention, states that when two particles are entangled and then separated miles apart from each other, they are still linked;

whereas when one is measured the other reacts instantaneously faster than the speed of light. There is still an apparent intelligent, energetic connection between them after the separation. Albert Einstein was freaked out by this and called it "spooky action at a distance." He could not explain how there was still an energetic communication between the two particles after they were separated and that made him very uncomfortable. I submit they were never disconnected at all once entangled for the first time and then separated.

Quantum entanglement, however, is very real in our twenty-first century world and I'll reiterate once more at the risk of sounding redundant, it is where we get wireless communication and the internet. Just because something can't be fully explained in the science world does not mean it can be dismissed. If it crosses over into the spirit realm then science needs to follow where the arrows lead. This is what numerous quantum physicists have been doing throughout the years. However, I would warn that they do so with God's spiritual protection, being fully girded with the whole armor of God in Christ Jesus (Eph. 6:10–18), as unless one is connecting with God through the Holy Spirit, contacting the quantum field is just another form of spirit medium mysticism, which Deuteronomy chapter 18 strictly forbids.

The following excerpt was taken from an interview with Cleve Backster by Derrick Jensen, published in *Sun*

*Magazine*. Backster referenced Rupert Sheldrake's work with dogs, described in the book *Dogs That Know when their Owners Are Coming Home* (1999):

"He puts a time recording camera on both the dog at home and the human companion at work. He has discovered that even if people come home from work at a different time each day, at the very moment the person leaves work, the dog at home heads for the door."

It seems that once a connection or entanglement between two people or two entities is made and agreed upon, then even at great distances that connection can be felt. You have heard of a mother in America whose daughter is halfway around the world when suddenly the mother gets this ill feeling that something is wrong with her daughter. She picks up the phone to call her, only to find out she had been in a car accident at the exact time the mother had that ill feeling about her. The daughter assures her mother she's ok, but the mother's intuition was rock solid. The mother felt that spiritual connection at the subatomic or intuitive level.

I found this next example of quantum entanglement in an article on LifeCoachCode.com entitled "New Research Shocks Scientists: Human Emotion Physically Shapes Reality."

"Three different studies, done by different teams of scientists proved something really extraordinary. But when a new research connected these three discoveries, something shocking was realized. Something hiding in plain sight."

Human emotion literally shapes the world around us. Not just our perception of the world, but reality itself.

In the first experiment, human DNA, isolated in a sealed container, was placed near a test subject. Scientists gave the donor emotional stimulus and fascinatingly enough, the emotions affected their DNA in the other room.

In the presence of negative emotions, the DNA tightened. In the presence of positive emotions, the coils of the DNA relaxed.

In the second, similar but unrelated experiment, a different group of scientists extracted leukocytes (white blood cells) from donors and placed them into chambers so they could measure electrical changes.

In this experiment, the donor was placed in one room and subjected to emotional stimulation consisting of video clips, which generated different emotions in the donor.

The DNA was placed in a different room in the same building. Both the donor and his DNA were monitored and as the donor exhibited emotional peaks or valleys (measured by electrical responses), the DNA exhibited the identical responses at the exact same time.

There was no lag time, no transmission time. The DNA peaks and valleys exactly matched the peaks and valleys of the donor in real time.

# INTENTION

The scientists wanted to see how far away they could separate the donor from his DNA and still get this effect. They stopped testing after they separated the DNA and the donor by fifty miles and still had the same result. No lag time—no transmission time.

The DNA and the donor had the same identical responses in time. The conclusion was that the donor and the DNA can communicate beyond space and time.

The third experiment proved something extremely shocking. Scientists observed the effect of DNA on our physical world. Light photons, which make up the world around us, were observed inside a vacuum. Their natural locations were completely random.

Human DNA was then inserted into the vacuum. Shockingly the photons were no longer acting random. They precisely followed the geometry of the DNA.

Scientists who were studying this, described the photons behaving "surprisingly and counter-intuitively." They went on to say that "We are forced to accept the possibility of some new field of energy!"

They concluded that human DNA literally shape the behavior of light photons that make up the world around us.

So, when new research was done and these three scientific claims were connected, scientists were shocked. They came to a stunning realization that if our emotions affect our DNA, and our DNA shapes the world around us, then our emotions physically change the world around us.

In sum, it's not that we are just connected to our DNA beyond space and time. We create our reality by choosing it with our feelings. Science has already proven some mind-blowing facts about the universe we live in. All we have to do is connect the dots."

You can do what you want with this information, and I'm in no way telling you what to believe, but it certainly opens the mind up to new possibilities with regards to outward human potential, beginning with inner human thought and intent.

Sources: https://www.youtube.com/watch?v=pq1q58w-Tolk; Science Alert;
Heart Math; Above Top HYPERLINK "http://www.abovetopsecret.com/forum/thread434438/pg1" HYPERLINK "http://www.abovetopsecret.com/forum/thread434438/pg1" HYPERLINK "http://www.abovetopsecret.com/forum/thread434438/pg1"Secret;
http://www.bibliotecapleyades.net/mistic/esp_gregg-braden_11.htm;

As I stated and explained, intention is one will, imposing itself onto another, but it gets more interesting than that. We've seen how dogs can tell when their owners intend to leave wherever they are and start their way home. Well, the next story will blow your mind as it did mine.

French researcher Rene Peoc'h has demonstrated experiments involving young chicks bonding to a robot instead of their mother (*Psychokinesis Experiments with Human and Animal Subjects upon a Robot Moving at Random*, 2002).

These freshly hatched chicks imprint on the first moving object they see upon being hatched, and then they follow it around. This imprinting instinct (or as I call it "Imprinstinct") causes them to bond with their mother when they are hatched. However, if this happens in an incubator, and the first moving thing they see is a person, then they latch onto that person as a result.

In his experiments, Peoc'h used a small robot that randomly moved around on wheels. The robot movements were determined by a random-number generator inside the robot and traced the random path out on the floor. Peoc'h exposed the newly hatched chicks to this robot, and they imprinted on it as if it were their mother. Peoc'h then put them in a cage so they could see the robot, but they were locked inside the cage and could not go to the robot. Instead they willed the robot to them.

The robot, after having been tested numerous times moving randomly around the room, was once again put on the floor and suddenly moved itself on over to the cage where the chicks were and stayed there. The chicks had to be near the robot and had somehow influenced the random-number generator. Amazingly, the robot had moved toward the cage and not in its random pattern around the room any longer. As an aside, chicks that were not imprinted on the robot had no effect on it. Apparently, the sheer power of the chicks' intention and deep love for their mother affected the robot on an energetic level. This confirms to me that thoughts and feelings are what I call spiritual atmospheric energy (SAE).

Subsequently, Peoc'h did another experiment with the other group of chicks that were not imprinted onto the robot after being hatched and therefore had no effect on it after being placed in the cage. He put those chicks back in the cage, shut the light out in the room and placed a small candle on top of the robot. The chicks then willed the random robot over to the cage so they could be closer to the light.

Another story I'd like to convey is one of spontaneous healing. The story of *Saturday Review* editor Norman Cousins (told in his book *Anatomy of an Illness: As Perceived by the Patient*, 1979) is one lesson we could all learn from. Proverbs 17:22 says, "A merry hearts works good like medicine, but a broken spirit dries the bones."

In 1964 and during the Cold War, Norm Cousins was admitted to a hospital for tests and treatments after a stressful trip to Russia. He was diagnosed with a debilitating illness known as Ankylosing Spondylitis that confined him to his bed. His condition deteriorated and he was given a gloomy prognosis. He noticed that the depressing routine of hospital life tended to produce side effects that aggravated his condition.

He laughed himself healthy again after checking out of the hospital (with the blessing of his doctor) and into a comfortable (yet less expensive) hotel where the food was much more pleasing to the taste and he could watch funny movies while he medicated himself with high doses of Vitamin C. He was convinced that the slow improvement in his condition was due to his individualized methods of therapy and having taken charge of his own situation.

In fact, he once said after being diagnosed with this illness that was killing him, "I realized that if sadness and sickness are hooked together, then happiness and health must also be hooked together."

Hence, it is all of this to simply point out the obvious, that man has a hidden power to exercise his intent to get what he wants in life. To add value to the world just by thinking and feeling sincerely about self and others. Then taking inspired action to bring about those good things!

My final example of the power of intention is my childhood friend and former bodybuilder Paul "Quadzilla" DeMayo. Growing up with Paul was great. He was one of the funniest and most charismatic people I've ever known. The following story about Paul was contributed by his brother, Mike DeMayo:

"As a young kid, Paul was always athletic and into sports. Whether it was Pop Warner Football, Little League or Babe Ruth Baseball, or even just street hockey or tag rush around the neighborhood, he was always into something. And along with being influenced by the typical mainstream athletes from major sports, he was also influenced by a couple of lesser known guys from the lesser known sport of body-building—Arnold Schwarzenegger and Lou Ferrigno. He was fascinated by the movie *Pumping Iron* (which featured both men) and became a huge fan of *The Incredible Hulk* TV show which starred Ferrigno. He admired those guys for their physique and got a gist for the work required to reach that level from the *Pumping Iron* movie.

After playing high school sports and graduating in 1985, he wanted to stay active athletically, so he turned to weight training. After a short time of putting in serious training, he started to see the results in his body. He worked out at Gold's Gym in Everett, Massachusetts, which was the biggest name gym in the area at that time and drew many competitive body builders from the area.

INTENTION

A lot of them encouraged Paul that he had a real shot to win if he trained hard and competed. And so, he did!

Along with working a full-time job, he did serious weight and cardio training and set his sights on winning body-building contests. Within a short time, he competed in some small contests and did well. By the summer of 1987 he got ready for the Mr. Teen Massachusetts Contest and won it at age nineteen. It was at that point that he decided to dedicate himself to training even more seriously and set his sights on eventually making it to the pro ranks.

Over the next seven years, he stuck with his training and competed in several national level contests. At the same time, he also got more and more exposure in the body-building industry and found his way into several body-building magazines and some ESPN TV spots. He was widely regarded as an up-and-comer in the sport. Training for contests was cyclical and sometimes his body was in peak condition and other times he just trained in maintenance mode. Paul always stuck to a very strict diet program and avoided many of the unhealthy eating habits that are more common to men in their late teens and early twenties. The road was not easy; there were setbacks such as injuries and losses at Nationals where he felt he looked his best. But he never quit, always rebounded and stuck to his goals, training even harder, and coming back for another shot at a professional world title.

Finally, in 1994, Paul broke through and won the NPC Men's Nationals. This win was the pinnacle of his career. He had finally reached the professional level he had been working towards and earned a great amount of respect across the industry and very quickly came to be known as "Quadzilla" with the biggest legs in pro body building. The up-and-comer had finally arrived. Along with earning his pro card, he was offered a lucrative sponsorship with Met-RX. With this endorsement money the company also gave him a dream car—a brand new metallic blue Corvette ZR1. He was on top of the world and was finally enjoying the fruits of his labor—the benefits of sticking to and achieving his goal!

Paul spent about a year or so after that as a pro competitor and competed in the European Grand Prix Tour as well as the Mr. Olympia Contest in 1995 before retiring from the sport."

GOOD THINGS ARE SUPPOSED TO HAPPEN TO YOU!

I personally grew up with Paul DeMayo and must say he was a dynamic personality. His presence introduced him before he ever opened his mouth. Not just physically which is obvious, but his glowing persona enhanced that. His personality literally created his personal reality.

Paul "Quadzilla" DeMayo, from Malden, Massachusetts, passed away on June 2, 2005. He was thirty-seven years old and died way before his time, but the point of this story is that Paul had an intention to be something definitive and his intention led him to accomplishing that end goal. Proving that the human Will and spirit is extremely powerful when directed solely at a specific purpose to the exclusion of all else. That type of concentrated energy is robust and can't be broken.

By now you've realized the obvious—that if you want something bad enough, chances are you will get it to one degree or another by sheer will and dogged determination. I have noticed in life that people tend to get more of what they intend or expect, because they believe—it's called faith.

REST IN PEACE, MY DEAR FRIEND
PAUL DeMAYO
09/12/67 – 06/02/05

## Chapter 6

# *Coming Attractions*

*If you don't believe that you can have the things in life your mind can imagine, then you need to revisit that and reprogram your mind until you do believe it.*

Albert Einstein said, "Imagination is the preview of life's coming attractions."

By using your imagination, you can change your destiny. You can do anything if you believe you can. It all starts with a thought, a dream, a vision. What do you dream about? What do you enjoy doing? What do you enjoy thinking about?

Are you writing down the answers to these questions? Take a few minutes and do that right now. Do you have different categories of these thoughts and dreams? Can you put together a list of ten dreams with three different categories?

How do you feel about these dreams? What kinds of emotions come to your mind when you think about these dreams?

This is the first stage of reprogramming your mind.

Are you with me so far?"

Without a vivid imagination you have not yet learned how to live a life filled with joy. If you don't believe that you can have the things in life your mind can imagine, then you need to revisit that and reprogram your mind until you do believe it. You can have just about any good thing you want in life, once you abandon the belief that you can't have it. If desire and imagination in and of itself were sinful, then we would not have that ability. We just need to be careful of what we desire, as there are a lot of things in life we would like to have, but they would do more harm to us than good.

Why does man have an imagination if not to envision and create what he wants to do moving forward in life? Anyone who tells you that you can't become what you can imagine does not realize that if you could not, then you would never be able to imagine it. Now, you may be thinking for example, "Well, I want to be able to jump off a mountain and fly like a bird without a parachute or a hang glider apparatus." I say, news flash, there's already a light bodysuit that was imagined by man that simulates bird wings and allows man to soar freely like a bird.

Or maybe you're thinking, "Well, I want to be invisible." I say that doesn't take but being antisocial and dressing in a bland way. People won't even notice you. However, there is quantum stealth body clothing that can literally make you invisible.

Remember, it always seems impossible until someone does it. God gave you imagination and ability to bring about what you can imagine, be it His will to allow or directly send it. The question is how bad do you want it?

The list of your thoughts, dreams, and visions are the foundation that will build your future. What do you want to do? What do you want to have? What do you want to be?

You will need to answer those questions in writing before we can move forward. Take your time with these questions, as your answers will change over time. Let's address each question. What do you want to do? About what? What do you desire to improve, learn, accomplish, etc. What do you want to have? What do you want to be?

If it could not be done at least to a modicum of success, then you'd never be able to imagine it. "With God all things are possible" (Matt. 19:26). The word *all* doesn't mean some or even most; it means *all*!

Now, man needs to be responsible with that imagination, but make no bones about it, if one person can achieve greatness in life, then you ought to be encouraged that *you* also can achieve greatness. In fact, I believe you should aspire to do so, as it will inspire everyone around you that they can too. There are way too many underachievers in life much to the chagrin I believe of Almighty God, but He has told us that through His Word, "We are not to be conformed to the pattern of this world (morally speaking), but be ye transformed by the renewing of your mind" (Romans 12:2).

To conform to the patterns of this world means to live decadently at the neglect of other's needs, which is what wealth is primarily for in God's eyes. Decadence literally means "moral decay" in the English language. The official definition states:

dec·a·dence 'dekədəns/*noun*
- moral or cultural decline as characterized by excessive indulgence in pleasure or luxury. "He denounced Western decadence."
- Synonyms:
- dissipation,degeneracy,debauchery,corruption,depravity,vice,sin, moral decay, immorality.

The question is how to go about achieving greatness? Well, it all begins with your thinking. God gave you a mental computer in your head that puts the world's largest super-computer to shame.

You just need to diligently reprogram it daily for a minimum of five minutes every morning upon awakening in meditation to think positive.

Never allow negativity into your mind. Be consciously aware of your unconscious negative thoughts, correct and replace them with your new positive affirmations.

Pretend that a six hundred-pound, eight-foot-high person is guarding and protecting your brain from negative thoughts. That person is keenly aware and senses when a negative thought is trying to enter the perimeter of his orbit. His job is to ward off the negative thought and then contact your positive affirmation team so they can counter it with a positive thought instead. You cannot have two thoughts at the same time.

This will take daily, moment-by-moment, conscious effort on your part. It's not as easy as it sounds, but easy enough if application is disciplined.

This means you need to stop watching the boob box and put on inspirational, motivational messages that teach you how to use your mind.

What are you doing? Why are you doing that activity? Does that activity help you achieve your goal? What are you willing or not willing to do to accomplish that goal?

Are you writing the answers down to these questions so that you can review them on a regular basis? Do that right now either in a notebook or on a sheet of paper.

I am willing to <u>blank</u> every morning.

I am willing to <u>blank</u> every day at lunchtime.

I am willing to <u>blank</u> every day after supper.

I am willing to <u>blank</u> before I go to bed.

Positive reprogramming is not only possible but necessary in order that you may experience the opposite of what you are experiencing now as a result of the previous faulty programming of your environment thus far in your life.

Here are some videos you should watch: Les Brown, Bob Proctor, Jack Canfield.

Here are some audio tapes you should listen to: John Kehoe, Bob Proctor, Steve Chandler.

Here are a few books you should read: The New Testament, *Think and Grow Rich*, *As a Man Thinketh*.

Here are a few web pages you should visit: YourYouniverse on YouTube, Dr. Charles Stanley on YouTube and Dave Ramsey on YouTube.

Have you ever done a YouTube video? Try doing one now with the goals you are trying to achieve.

Good Things Are Supposed To Happen To You!

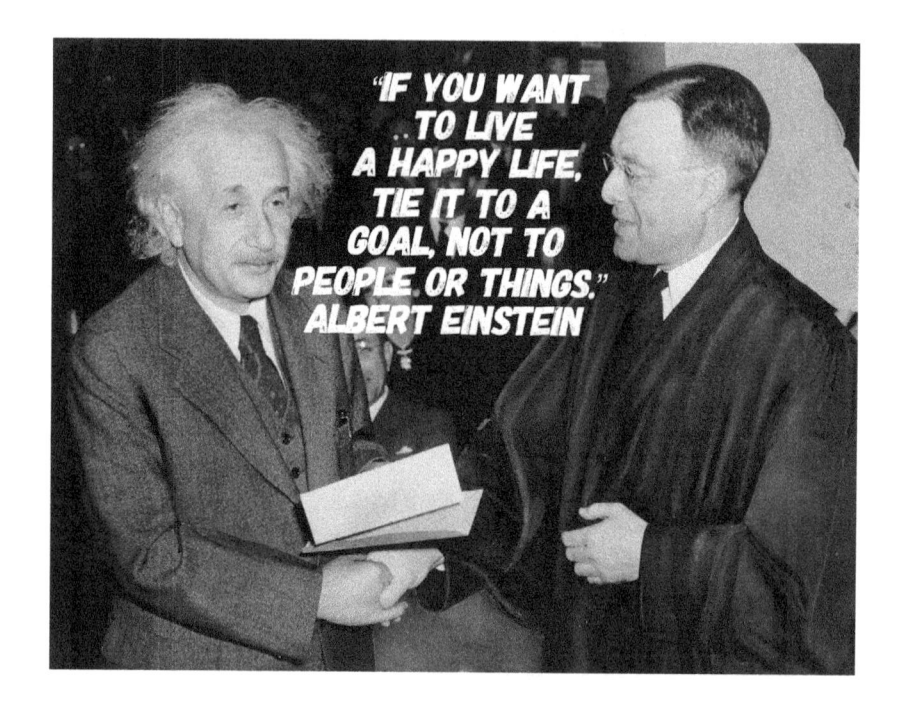

"IF YOU WANT TO LIVE A HAPPY LIFE, TIE IT TO A GOAL, NOT TO PEOPLE OR THINGS."
ALBERT EINSTEIN

## Chapter 7

# *You Were Once Dead*

*Every single day, you have about sixteen hours of awake time. That's sixteen hours to inspire, motivate or teach at least one person—sixteen hours to make a difference in someone's life including your own.*

You were dead for billions of years before you were ever alive. Therefore, you were born for a reason. God never ever does anything that is random. If God came to you and you asked Him, "Father, did you Create me to be average?" What do you think His answer would be?

There are seven billion people on this earth right now. Why are you here now? You are here for a purpose.

By now you realize what a ridiculous and rhetorical question that is. Of course, He would say to you resoundingly, "No! I created you for my good pleasure to be saved from the penalty of your sin first and foremost (Jn 3:3; 1 Jn 3:4). Secondly, as Jesus said, 'I created you that you may have life and that more abundantly' (Jn 10:10), so that you could become the best version of yourself that I Created you to be. Not to fit into some average cookie cutter mold that man has made for himself, so he wouldn't have to rise any higher than anybody else. That's just a waste of individual creativity and raw talent. That was never my intention for mankind. That is boring. I created you to inspire others, to motivate them and to teach love everywhere you go by showing love. Love is contagious and infectious! It's like manure; when you pile it up in one place it stinks. When you spread it around it makes things grow!"

Let's get to work. What are your priorities? What do you want to happen now? What do you need to do within the next five minutes, five days, five weeks and five months? Are you writing these answers down? Time is precious. How are you allotting your time to meet your daily goals?

If that thought about what God would say to you, along with these questions doesn't make you re-evaluate your existence, then there is no hope for you. However, we're going to just move along here as though you are indeed reevaluating your life and that it is the reason you are reading this book. I want you to consider something as you are reading this. Every single day you have about sixteen hours of awake time. That's sixteen hours to inspire, motivate or teach at least one person—sixteen hours to make a difference in someone's life including your own.

Do you consciously consider that each morning upon awakening? If not, you can start now. Put a Post-it note reminder on your bathroom mirror to remind yourself until it becomes an automatic thought. It takes a minimum of thirty days to see a difference in your attitude and outlook on life, but it will become automatic before long if you consistently do this every morning. Remember, you don't stop lifting weights once you reach your fitness goal to look a certain way. You keep lifting in order to maintain and improve on it. If you stop lifting, your body stops responding positively and starts to let go of its fitly shape. Neglect your body and your body will only affirm that neglect. See, life, like your body, is responding to what you put into it.

We are what we repeatedly do. Therefore, excellence is a habit. What are your daily thought habits? What are your daily action habits? Write them down in a notebook or on a sheet of paper.

## Chapter 8

## *Reprogram your Mind*

———————•———————

*Your autonomic subconscious mind is something also known as a Paradigm.*

*Y*ou possess the ability to reprogram your mind by a principle called autosuggestion. Autosuggestion consists of simple commands that you plant in your own subconscious mind daily, like a farmer planting seeds in a field of soft, fertile soil.

Your subconscious mind does not think for itself. It is the automatic system that is your body. Your heart beats automatically and your brain computes automatically. Archibald MacLeish once said, "The only thing about a man that is a man is his mind. Everything else (internal organs etc.) you can find inside a pig or a horse."

Your intelligent mind is the only thing that separates you from the rest of God's creation. Again, the fact that a bunch of cells can think about thinking, and then think about thinking about thinking is the most fascinating thing to me. There are levels upon levels upon levels of conscious thinking. It is literally a mindboggling matrix.

Your autonomic subconscious mind is something also known as a paradigm, which is simply a bunch of habits formed in our minds from the formative years of youth by the people who raised us. We are the sum-total of other people's thoughts, ideas and beliefs until we are old enough, intellectually able and so inclined to form our own. The good news is the majority, of your paradigm can be reprogrammed. The rest is inherently genetic, which is why we look like our parents, sound like them, walk like them, etc.

The fact that you have the power (and yes, I call that power, because it is a powerful thing) to change how you think if you really want to, is a major league breakthrough. The things you can imagine becoming are limitless. Your subconscious mind will eventually begin to construct the world around you according to your paradigm. Just look at the results of your life thus far. Now consider your thought patterns. They determine every one of your decisions good, bad or indifferent and therefore your results. Want different results? Change your thought patterns.

Earlier we talked about what a paradigm is. Now you are going to learn what you can accomplish by reprogramming your mind to form a new paradigm. There was a man who was well on his way from gutter to glory in just ninety days when he learned he could change his life by simply changing his attitude of mind. The moment he began to shift how he viewed himself and his circumstances, both he and those circumstances began to change.

This was the breakthrough this man needed. Make no bones about it, change always starts with you, how you view yourself, the world and your place in the world. My dad always drilled it home to me when I was growing up. He would always expound, "Ace, attitude of gratitude is everything in life. It determines your altitude."

I didn't quite understand the depth of those words until I became a grown man in my early forties and had my own paradigm shift. At this point I understood that a spirit of gratitude is the most magnetic force a person could possess. It will get you everywhere in a world where people are heavily medicated and could not be bothered to think. I was now learning how to use my mind to help myself and others.

## Chapter 9

# *A Grateful Heart*

---

*A grateful heart helps you to remain
reachable and teachable, always learning.*

The attitude of gratitude is one of the more popular platitudes out there, and a platitude is simply a principle condensed into a memorable saying or talking point. This saying in-particular has so much truth in it. A grateful heart will make you stronger in your spirit, which is your thoughts and ideas that lead to your words and actions (your mind is the spirit world). Your spirit can affect others in this way. For example; music is a spirit which can alter how you feel in any given moment. A grateful heart will make you deeper in your soul (the seat of your emotions, which are created by your thoughts) with empathy.

A grateful heart is one of the most magnetic spirits you can project. It helps you to remain reachable and teachable, always learning. It is magnetic in that a person with a grateful heart has positive thoughts which vibrate at a high frequency. It attracts everyone and everything on that same positive frequency, like tuning in to your favorite radio station.

There is a saying: "Your energy introduces you before you ever open your mouth." Ever see someone walk into a room and their aura just glows about them? It literally emanates from them. That is their spiritual atmospheric energy field (SAE). Their thoughts are high positive thoughts that are creating the magnetic glow you see around their being. It all begins with gratitude, which helps one to keep a consistent high mood. My dad used to say, "If you want to walk with high people you've got to keep a high mood." As a teenager I thought he was sanctioning.... well, on second thought we won't go there (laughing).

Aura is not only visible in some people, but also sensed quite prevalently. One night my girlfriend and I were having a glass of wine at a local venue where I do public performances a couple of times a year. The mood of the moment changed when these two guys walked in and we sensed a vibe that was as negative a vibe as I'd sensed in a long time. They never even made eye contact with us but just sat down across the bar to order a drink. I felt a strong negative energy emanating from them and said to my girl, "Come on, baby, let's go home." We then got up and exited the establishment.

Now, just the opposite is true for positive people who have such a glow about them that not only can you feel their vibe, but you literally see it. So much that it completely fills the room with a glow and all attention is on them. They are so magnetic that everybody either wants to know who they are or simply can't take their eyes off them. Vibrations are very powerful and generated by thought, feeling and intent in a person's being.

How do we know people are spiritual energy first before anything of solid matter? Take a set of identical twin girls. One is average to slightly low on the energy scale, while the other is very happy, energetic, and positive. A baby sees both when they walk in the door together but is taken to the more positive, high-energy one. It doesn't take an engineering degree to figure out why. Be ever mindful of how and what you are projecting—the energy you're vibrating. It either attracts or repels people and people can't get through life successfully without the right people in their lives.

Remember, thoughts are SAE, or spiritual atmospheric energy, and energy facilitates/becomes matter when concentrated and determined enough. Your energy level and consistency will determine what manifests/shows up in your life. You see it every day in people's lives, depending on what mindset and energy level they vibrate at. Ever notice how high energy people just seem to make positive and exciting things happen? Life positively responds to them.

Negative energy vibrates at a low frequency. Positive energy vibrates at a high frequency. Both are magnetic and attract like energy. Think about those people you know that are always talking about the things they do not want in their life. Constantly complaining of how they are a victim and the bad things that happen to them. You guessed it, they create and invite/attract more of those things into their life. Life affirms their beliefs and responds negatively to them. Especially in crisis situations that can permanently alter or even end their life, unless God steps in to prevent it for future reasons that only He knows about.

Well, the opposite is true for the positive person who is always talking good about others. Talking about his dreams and goals and always blessing people with whom he makes contact. Speaking of how he's a millionaire with opportunity and how he is making the best of what he's been given to help others in life. What happens to that person? Well, like a ship with an address coordinate punched into its navigation system, 99.9999% of the time he gets to his destination. He achieves his goals. It's that simple. Be consistently positive daily without fail and you will manifest positive things in your life.

You will never be able to live this moment again, so start the day by seeing richness and fullness in everything, in everyone around you and in everything you do today. Take five quiet minutes and create your day to detail in your mind as to how you want it to play out, barring any unforeseen happenings which you will take in stride and with grace. If you plan and create your day saying to yourself that you will respond to anything negative with gratitude for the blessings in your life, then you mostly will. Your subconscious mind will give you then what you train and re-program it for now, and each moment moving forward.

## Chapter 10

## *Mental Pharmacy*

---

*What you think about daily is what you will become.*

There was a study done on two groups of patients. Half were given real medication to heal them, and the other group was given a sugar pill but thought they were being given real medicine. Both groups experienced healing. So, what happened to the second group? Why were they healed when they were only given a sugar pill? The second group believed the medicine given to them would heal them even though it wasn't real medicine.

This shows us that healing primarily comes not only either directly from God or the healing process He has set into motion in the universe, but from the belief that one will be healed. The belief inside of a person is the solidified emotional conviction of the thoughts that agree with their deep seeded philosophies. Human thought comes from the very subatomic substance and subsistence of what and who created every tangible thing in nature. "Now faith is confidence in what we hope for and assurance about what we do not see." (Heb 11:1).

*I once read a story ("De La Philosophie Et De La Longevite," by Dr. Pinaud) about a cook at a large dinner party who ran out from the kitchen and screamed, "Stop eating! I accidentally mixed arsenic in the food!" Several people were immediately doubled over with pains and became ill, which only halted when the cook came back out to say it was a false alarm and that he was mistaken.

Why did the patrons feel sick with pains if it wasn't arsenic? The imagination and power of suggestion is extremely potent, but human thoughts can create chemicals in the body that can literally make us ill.

Be careful of your thoughts. They create the ideas you believe and your personality, which in turn "creates your personal reality" (to quote one of my favorite experts on the topic of spontaneous healing in neuroscience, Dr. Joe Dispenza). Train your mind to think mostly positive and you will have good ideas, which will form beliefs of wellness. You will therefore be a happy person with more healthy, happy friends and life circumstances. Happy people are healthy people and healthy people are happy people.

Your beliefs affect you profoundly and daily. Thoughts create chemicals in the human mind that then travel throughout the body either harming or healing it. Cortisol is a stress hormone chemical the body creates and releases when under great stress. It is the leading cause of almost all degenerative diseases.

Now, collocate that with the endorphin hormone chemical the body releases when we think happy thoughts, which create happy feelings. Endorphins boost the immune system to fight off disease and sickness while cortisol in abundance attacks the immune system and weakens it.

We ought to be careful of the thoughts we think and obsess over. Obsessing over good things like your goals and dreams is a healthy thing and will gravitate those things toward you as you move toward them. Like your mirror image moves toward you as you move toward it.

What you think about daily is what you will become. Your subconscious mind does not know the difference whether you're mentally experiencing something or literally experiencing it. Therefore, it will create the neuron memory connections in your frontal lobe as if you are literally experiencing it. Dr. Joe Dispenza says, "Neurons that fire together wire together."

This teaches us that mental rehearsal in every aspect of our lives is extremely important in achieving any and every goal we set for ourselves. You've got to consistently, passionately and vividly dream it in detail first before it ever becomes a tangible reality in your life, which reminds me of the platitude "Thoughts Become Things"—eventually. If you don't know where you're going how will you ever get there? If you don't know what you want how will you ever get it? You need to move forward with definiteness of purpose. Once you define the what, the how will develop out of your devotion and commitment to it.

## CHAPTER 11

# *From the Inside Out*

―❖―

*It all begins in your mind. Learn to utilize the mind God gave you and your outside circumstances will change when your energy changes.*

Most people are mental slaves to their environment, instead of learning to make their environment a slave to their mind. Let me explain. What you obsessively plant into your subconscious mind daily eventually begins to construct around you. Example: bestselling author Jack Canfield (*Chicken Soup for the Soul*) told a story about how he was perplexed over his cat who had feline leukemia, and the doctors told him there was no cure for it.

Well, this was in the background of Jack's mind, and one day he came across information about a seminar on how to earn more money, which was the opposite of what Jack and his wife were all about. Nevertheless, he felt drawn to this seminar for some reason, and having learned to trust his instincts, he decided to go and see what it was all about.

> He sat next to this woman, and they got to talking. He told her what he did for work and she told him she was a veterinarian who specialized in (of all things) feline leukemia. Jack said, "Really? My cat has leukemia. Doctors said there's no cure."

She told him there was now a cure because of recent breakthroughs. They exchanged cards, and working with Jack's veterinarian, she cured his cat.

Either Jack's subconscious mind, God Himself or God working through Jack's subconscious mind led him to this seminar to meet this woman who then healed his cat. His life literally began to construct around him in not only this instance but many other seemingly weird coincidences.

When you have a definiteness of purpose, you will most definitely achieve the end of that purpose. It is in achievement that you inspire others and realize your purpose for adding value to this world. Napoleon Hill, in his book *Think and Grow Rich*, said, "Whatever the mind can conceive and believe it can achieve." It's all around you every day. You just need to pay attention. Pick one thing you really want to do in life and obsess over it daily.

Start in the morning right when you wake up. Be thankful in advance and pray diligently for your goal. Speaking the affirmation that you have already achieved and received it. Then thank God for that blessing upon you. After about thirty to ninety days or so your subconscious mind will begin to believe that you indeed have already achieved it (so long as you don't entertain old negative thought tapes that have played over and over in your mind for years. You've got to be mindful of that every day). It will then begin to slowly construct and manifest around you. In other words, it will all start coming together for you.

It may take two months or two years, but if you do not quit you will eventually achieve what you perceive. The more passionate you are about it the higher you will vibrate, and the quicker you will achieve it. Personally, I believe God has His hand in this, but others simply believe it is their subconscious mind at work. That which I say God created and uses to bring about things that are not yet, as though they already are. It is man's faith that interacts with conscious reality and fuels it. Jesus said to the leper, "Rise and go; your faith has made you well" (Luke 17:19). The Leper's healing came from within. Hebrews 11:1 says, "Now faith is confidence in what we hope for and assurance about what we do not see."

It all begins in your mind. Learn to utilize the mind God gave you and your outside circumstances will change when your energy changes, but you need to say your affirmations daily and write them down, even if you don't believe them at first. This is your time of planting or sowing these seeds into your subconscious mind so that you can reap the harvest of your dreams. As Dr. Charles Stanley once wrote, "Remember, you reap what you sow, more than you sow, later than you sow. This principle applies to everyone, both Christians and Non-Christians. It is irrevocable. There is no escape. It is the Law of Life."

Even though you may not believe at first that you can have or achieve the things in life you desire, eventually you will believe it once your subconscious mind is convinced of it. So long as God allows it according to His plan for your life, but once your subconscious believes in something, you then start acting like it and everything you do moves in the direction of that belief.

This is the reason I strongly agree with the Word of God in that my desires be in line with His plan for my life or at least headed toward the cross and not away from it. God will ultimately show me the specific plan as I move toward His light.

I certainly do not want to start believing something God does not want for me, as it would not be good for me, hence the old saying, be careful what you wish for; you just might get it. After all, what God blesses you with will be so much more fulfilling than anything you could ever imagine for yourself. For He is your Maker and knows what makes you tick far better than you do. In Psalms 139:13–16, King David said, " For you created my inmost being; you knit me together in my mother's womb. I praise you because I am fearfully and wonderfully made; your works are wonderful. I know that full well. My frame was not hidden from you when I was made in the secret place, when I was woven together in the depths of the earth. Your eyes saw my unformed body; all the days ordained for me were written in your book before one of them came to be."

You just need to believe Jesus when He said, "Ask and it shall be given you; Seek and ye shall find; Knock and it shall be opened unto you." In Matt 6:31-33 Jesus said, "So do not worry, saying, 'What shall we eat?' or 'What shall we drink?' or 'What shall we wear?' For the pagans run after all these things, and your heavenly Father knows that you need them. But seek first his kingdom and his righteousness, and all these things will be given to you as well."

Once you believe the Good Lord and His Holy Word, your faith will only get stronger.

## Chapter 12

## *Always Smile*

---

*You need to see yourself in your mind as happy and smiling before you can be happy, so putting on a smile, even if it's fake, can help you feel better.*

Remember this and never forget it: no matter what kind of mood you may be in, whenever the camera is on you—always smile! Your face in a picture is frozen in time forever and you don't want people seeing you without that infectious grin. More importantly, you don't want people thinking you're an unhappy person. That will defeat the purpose of your existence, which is to add value to others who observe and confirm your existence. To inspire another is to fulfill them.

One day my Fiancée's nine-year-old daughter (twelve now) who is a happy, bubbly little kid and always smiling, was taking a picture with her mom and little sister. As I was going to take the picture, I noticed she was frowning because her mom had just told her "NO" about something.

I said to her, "Smile, sunshine! You have a beautiful smile and should always show it to the world. Especially in a picture. See, once the picture is taken, it's frozen in time forever. Always show your happy side in pictures regardless of how you are feeling in the moment. Even though it's a fake smile in that moment, it reflects you overall in that picture as the happy person you are ninety-nine percent of the time." After all, we snap pictures to capture good moments, right? I mean, nobody really wants to capture a bad moment in a picture only to be reminded of it later in life, unless the joke was on them and they have a good sense of humor? Many a good laugh has been had flipping through old photo albums with family and seeing someone crying. Especially when they remember why the person was crying in that moment way back when (Laughing).

Now she and her little sister always smile when the camera is on them, no matter what they're feeling, because they understand this principle.

When you're feeling down try smiling, even if you do not feel like it. Most times smiling can change your mood. Like visualizing something before it happens. You can't build a new home unless you first visualize it, then have it drawn up by an architect. A good ole song you love that conjures up an old memory and the feelings that go with it can make you smile. It can turn your whole day around.

You need to see yourself in your mind as happy and smiling before you can be happy, so putting on a smile even if it's fake, can help you feel better. I call that "vivid visualization." We manifest what we visualize. We visualize, realize, actualize, and materialize.

## Chapter 13

## *Manifold Manifest*

---

*Dreams are the colors of life. Dreams motivate, move, and behoove you to get up out of bed early every morning to seize the day.*

The more vivid and detailed your visualization, the more manifold your manifest will be. If you have a small dream, then you will only manifest a small dream.

It doesn't take any more energy or time to dream a big dream than it does a small dream and big dreams have power, so *dream big!*

Dreams are the colors of life. Dreams motivate, move and behoove you to get up out of bed early every morning to seize the day. To pray and meditate on your daily life affirmations and aspirations. Then get out there into the world and make things happen in your life for the benefit of self and others.

We live in the most affluent, opulent country the world has ever known. The United States of America is a place where people can afford to pay you handsomely for your product or ideas. Try pushing your talent in a third world country where the citizen majority vibrates on a low frequency and has no money to buy anything. You could be the best salesperson on the planet and make no money there, because there is no money in those countries.

We here in America are millionaires with opportunity. We have every money-making tool at our disposal and yet there are more people living off the government than you could shake an EBT card at. Why? People don't know how to think. The boob tube has marvelously dumbed down the masses in this country.

People love innovation and you have the mind to be innovative. As of 2017 there are about eleven million millionaires in America, according to Spectrem Group's *Market Insights Report* and that number is growing. That is nothing to sneeze at. Why not you? It all starts with your thinking. All energy starts with a thought. Thoughts generate feelings and feelings generate vibration. Good positive vibrations attract good, positive people. The same goes for negative vibrations. They attract negative people and situations. It is that simple. Negative thoughts can never yield you a positive, successful life.

Your current thought pattern has literally manifested the life you now experience, because it's what you believe about yourself—life circumstances notwithstanding. I know people who grew up poor with nothing and became very wealthy. If you are not happy with life as you know it, change your thought and action patterns for a better life experience. Your thoughts literally become things, but you must pick a path and move forward toward a goal. Then the people and circumstances will develop around you to bring about that goal. They will literally move quicker toward you the quicker and more determined you are moving toward that goal.

God gave you an imagination. Use it to envision your future. Again, Albert Einstein said this: "Imagination is everything! Your imagination is the preview of life's coming attractions!" If you do not imagine, you will never manifest a single good thing in this life unless it's by direct blessing from God in His Divine Grace. Which is designed to lead you unto repentance but remember, even a broken clock is right twice a day and as Tom Petty sang, "Even the losers get lucky sometimes."

Every masterpiece, every skyscraper, every love song ever written was once an imaginative thought in someone's mind. Hold onto what you want definitively and do not divert from it. If you keep changing your mind about what you want, you'll never generate enough high positive energy toward achieving anything and will end up with nothing.

## Chapter 14

# *The Law of Giving and Receiving*

*When you circulate your blessings that you no longer use, you are giving back.*

I got a message from a female friend of mine who said, "I noticed you're selling all your stuff. I just want to make sure you're ok?"

I laughingly replied, "Of course! I'm just making room for better blessings in my life. The law of giving and receiving says to get rid of things you no longer use so others who may be less fortunate can have the opportunity to enjoy them also, and to make room for the better things you couldn't afford before to come into your life. Thank you for your concern, however."

I thought that was funny, but I could see how she would think that, not being fully informed about what I was doing. The way the economy works, literally and spiritually, is that if you hoard good things and don't use them—like clothes, electronics, etc.—then you're not being a good steward with the blessings you already have.

In order to keep the cycle of giving and receiving moving uninterrupted, you need to recycle what you no longer use. Others who will use them can be blessed by them and those resources won't be wasted. Instead they will be passed on in the blessing cycle and not end up at the city dump.

It also opens-up space to receive blessings that are more useful to you at this time in your life. When you circulate the blessings you no longer use, you're giving back. Now, I'm not saying you should give away expensive items, unless of course you feel moved to do so, but selling them at a discount allows people with less money to purchase something of high value at a really good price. Something you may have paid top dollar for and taken care of that they could never afford. The idea is to keep the law of blessing flowing freely.

Luke12:15–21 tells us,

"Then he (Jesus) said to them, "Watch out! Be on your guard against all kinds of greed; life does not consist in an abundance of possessions." And he told them this parable: "The ground of a certain rich man yielded an abundant harvest, He thought to himself, 'What shall

## The Law Of Giving And Receiving

I do? I have no place to store my crops.' "Then he said, 'This is what I'll do. I will tear down my barns and build bigger ones, and there I will store my surplus grain. And I'll say to myself, "You have plenty of grain laid up for many years. Take life easy; eat, drink and be merry." "But God said to him, 'You fool! This very night your life will be demanded from you. Then who will get what you have prepared for yourself?' "This is how it will be with whoever stores up things for themselves but is not rich toward God."

Powerful words and a powerful lesson in adding value to the world by blessing others the way God would have us do so. When we better ourselves individually and earn more money, we are then able to help the less fortunate in a mighty way. That should be a person's motive for becoming wealthy. To further the Kingdom of Heaven on Earth.

## Chapter 15

## *Always Say Yes*

---

*When people offer you good things out of the kindness of their hearts, they are planting seeds with you so they can reap their own harvest down the road elsewhere.*

When someone offers you good things no matter what they are, say yes unless it's someone trying to keep you on the hook with a continuous guilt trip (obviously), always saying that you owe them. Here's why you say yes; when people offer you good things out of the kindness of their heart, they are planting seeds with you (whether they realize it or not), so they can reap their own harvest down the road elsewhere.

You do not have to feel guilty like you owe them something. You could simply say something like "Thank you so much for that generous token of kindness. It means a lot to me and I'm going to pay that forward to keep your blessing flowing."

That person will be repaid by the law of giving and receiving/sowing and reaping. You are the fertile soil for their seed planting, and it ought to make you smile and feel good that you are a big part of the cycle of goodness in this world.

See, the more seeds you plant the more bountiful your harvest will be, which is why Jesus said, "It is better to give than to receive." He wasn't saying that receiving was a bad thing. In fact, it's the other half of the law of reciprocity, aka, what goes around comes around. He was teaching the principle of the harvest, because again as the saying goes, you reap what you sow, more than you sow, later than you sow.

Saying no to someone who offers you good things is not being humble; it's literally insulting to them whether you realize that or not. Love is powerful and people often show their love by gift giving, which comes in many forms year-round, not just at Christmas, birthdays, and other special occasions.

So now you see how important it is to always say yes and how you play a big role in other people's seed planting. When you say no, you may be hindering your own blessings by as much as 50%, because you're interrupting the ebb and flow of the law of blessing. You don't ever want to do that in your life. You'll only be cheating yourself and others who express their love by giving you good things.

It's personal sabotage and God didn't create that universal law for you to interrupt it. He created it for you to be able to prosper like any good father would want for his children. Imagine if you went to give your child a gift out of the love in your heart and they rejected it? Think of how that would make you feel. You would feel hurt, like they did not love you and as if they were rejecting your love. You know they do love you, but the feeling still hurts the same. Therefore, always say yes.

## Chapter 16

# *One, Two, Three Punch*

———✦———

*Desire + Visualization and Affirmation=Success.*

In her 1962 publication *Dynamic Laws of Prosperity*, Catherine Ponder wrote, "Desire + Visualization and Affirmation = Success. The brain works in terms of mental images, so whatever images it has are likely to become reality at some point. Helping you to literally see your way to success." To reiterate, those mental images will literally construct your world around you as you see it in your mind.

The energy released by the passion of your thoughts will draw the people you need to help facilitate your career or whatever end you are determined toward. You often see this on a negative level with people who constantly seem to attract bad seeds and negative circumstances to themselves and then complain how they can't figure out why it keeps happening to them. If you are one of those people you now have your answer.

Now, look at this principle from a positive standpoint. Think about those people who just have that Midas touch. Everything they touch seems to blossom like a beautiful rose. This is proof that your thoughts literally construct your world around you by either drawing in positive people and circumstances like a vortex or repelling them and attracting just the opposite. Be consciously aware of your thought patterns, because at the end of each day you have nobody but you to blame for your misfortune. Not God, not the president, not the governor, not the mayor, not your boss, not your parents, not your friends, not your significant other, not your kids, nor even your pet. Nobody but *you*, so shift your thoughts and attitude toward life. Turn them positive, inward, and upward. Then you will see your circumstances begin to change for the better.

If you feel passionately about what you want, before long you'll see it begin to manifest from these directions. This is the reason it's so important for you to make the time every morning to do some work on your mental paradigm to reprogram it.

The first twenty minutes after you wake up are the most important, because your mind is most impressionable, as it's only working between about ten and twelve wave cycles per second when you first wake up. Anywhere from eight to twelve wave cycles per second is known as the alpha wave stage. It has been called the gateway to the subconscious mind according to scientific studies (https://mentalhealthdaily.com/2014/04/15/5-types-of-brain-waves-frequencies-gamma-beta-alpha-theta-delta/). Therefore, it's so important to put on something inspirational and motivational to set the spirit and tone for the rest of your day. To say your daily affirmations while they can sink deeply into your subconscious, before your mind has a chance to enter the high beta wave stage and the cluttered rat race, with all its gobbledygook that threatens to zap your positive energy.

You must get your mind to a point where you look forward to doing personal mind work every day and even multiple times a day. I love it because I know the sky is the limit as to the change I can bring about in my own life, just by emotional, repetitive thinking and reading God's mind on life through His Holy Word. I understood that if I could change my thoughts, my life would change. I find it extremely fascinating. In fact, and I've said it before, I haven't been this excited about learning new knowledge since my studies in theological seminary. This is where true spiritual change comes as a result of being "Born Again" by the power of God's Holy Spirit, according to the Gospel of Jesus Christ in John 3:3–7, Mark 16:16, and Acts 2:38–41.

If you ever want to realize these mental paradigm principles in this book to maximum potential, then do yourself a favor and enter a personal relationship with the Lord Jesus Christ. Then you'll see real spiritual power. This is where I part from mind powers mentors like Dr. Joe Dispenza, who encourage tapping into the quantum field (or the unified field) by way of mystic transcendental meditation.

The Bible clearly teaches that is demonic in Deuteronomy chapter 18, but a lot of these scientists are teaching that it is the one thing that finally unites all the religions of the world. I say that is pure poppycock.

With all due respect to these doctors and other experts, I believe that God is not some universal force that people just empty their minds, tap into and order what they want like ordering off a menu at the North Ave. Diner in Wakefield, Massachusetts. We serve an objective, intelligent Creator-God, specifying who He is and showing us His definitive Holy character throughout Scripture.

God is a person. In fact, He is one God in three persons—namely God the Father, God the Son, and God the Holy Spirit.

1John 5:7 states "For there are three that testify (in heaven), the Spirit, the water and the blood; and the three are in agreement" (KJV says "Are One"). Moses refers to this in Gen 1:26, "Let us make Man in our image in our likeness."

God has a consistency in His Holy character summed up in the Ten Commandments as described in Exodus 20, of which every human being can identify and agree with.

## ONE, TWO, THREE PUNCH

If all religions taught the same thing about God's character then I'd agree that quantum physics ties it together spiritually, but they do not. One religion teaches you can die in a jihad and go to heaven to enjoy sex with seventy vestal virgins (in other words, women will be sex slaves in heaven), while another teaches child sacrifice and yet another teaches marriage to multiple women including underage girls and on and on it goes. There is a huge moral discrepancy between the different religions of the world and the diverse sects thereof.

It's disgusting, the human atrocities some of these religions teach and allow, so I wholeheartedly do not agree that all religions lead to heaven, nor do I agree that quantum physics ties all religions together through the quantum field at the subatomic level (quantum entanglement). In fact, I personally see this universal god as the evil one himself and unless you're praying to God in Jesus's name via the Holy Spirit, connecting with the unified quantum field is nothing less than trafficking with demons. The science of quantum entanglement is real, but we must discern it very carefully as it is the spirit world.

Remember, there are two spirits in this world. There's God in Christ Jesus and

there's Satan, the evil one. Again, if you're not praying to God in Jesus's name through the Holy Spirit, then guess who you're connecting with when you enter meditative prayer?

## Chapter 17

## *Hitler Got away with It*

*There's a saying "The best type of leader is the one who shows you where to look, but not what to see." To me there must be a supreme moral Creator who will mercifully, righteously, and justly judge original sin and the personal sins of each man on the other side....*

A lot of people believe in the philosophy that says there's no right or wrong, only learning experiences. I do not. If there is no objective moral standard by which to call anything right or wrong, then morality is merely situation ethics. It is merely subjective, which means if I rob you at gunpoint to steal your wallet so I can get a bite to eat that I don't starve, then I'm not morally wrong in doing so because I can justify it. Even though you would probably beg to differ.

## HITLER GOT AWAY WITH IT

Furthermore, if there is no objective standard of right and wrong, then tyrants like Hitler got away with it. Think about it, Hitler kills six million Jews (that we know of), ruins countless millions of families, then shoots himself in the head, killing himself before being made to answer for it *in this life* and that's it? Does he not have to pay for what he did on the other side of the veil? Is there no perfect justice for his countless victims? Come on now! If you believe that, I'm selling a piece of ocean-front property in Fargo, North Dakota. You interested? Didn't think so.

The human conscience screams out for justice, while order and righteousness in the universe logically demands it. Otherwise nothing in this life would make any sense at all and there could not be a perfectly moral and just Creator named God in a place called Heaven if that were the case.

After all my studies, including seven years of formal theological seminary training, I know this beyond a shadow of a doubt: if the Bible is false regarding sin, the human condition, Jesus Christ, and eternal salvation, then nothing really matters. Being moral doesn't matter, doing the right thing doesn't matter, honoring your parents and fellow man doesn't matter, or anything else for that matter. None of it matters because when all is said and done and we die, there will be nothing on the other side waiting for us anyway. So, we may as well live it up as much as we can here in this life, because when it's over, it's over.

However, if the Bible is *true*, then nothing else matters when all is said and done, compared to what Jesus did for mankind. It doesn't matter who wins the Super Bowl, who wins "Dancing with the Stars," who wins "American Idol," etc. None of this will amount to anything more than a hill of horse dung in God's economy come Judgment Day. The only question God will ask each individual man and woman on that day is this: "What did you do with Jesus and the eternal salvation I offered you freely so that you could receive my eternal pardon, escaping the eternal penalty and punishment of your sin/high moral crimes (unrighteousness) against God and High Holy Heaven?"

Now, I'm merely giving you the biblical view of God and His mind on sin and the human condition. You, as the reader, will have to make your own choice on what to believe about God and who He is. That is a personal choice nobody can ever force you to make one way or the other.

There's a saying: The best type of leader is the one who shows you where to look, but doesn't tell you what to see. To me there must be a supreme moral Creator who will mercifully, righteously, and justly judge original sin and the personal sins of each man on the other side. It just makes sense to me.

Anything less gives no reasonable answer/response to the evil done in the flesh by rotten people who choose to inflict pain upon the innocent among us who wish to do no harm to others, but only live in peace. Now, I understand that none of us are perfectly innocent. We have all made mistakes in life and even bad decisions when we are angry or hurt, so I'm not saying there are any perfect people in the world, least of all me. Just different degrees of sin, depending on a person's disposition, personality and predisposition to it.

I'm merely pointing out that the quantum/unified field is not some magical plain where we all connect with the same God singing "Kumbaya," and like some magical genie we make wishes and He grants us those wishes. Just because people of all religions or no religion at all, possess the ability to tap into this healing and blessing energy it does not mean they are right with God and that his healing and blessing in their life is tantamount to automatic salvation. In Romans 2:4, Paul says, "Or do you show contempt for the riches of his kindness, forbearance and patience, not realizing that God's kindness is intended to lead you to repentance?"

The Bible clearly teaches that no matter what religion you are, if you live in harmony with the laws of the universe that God set in motion, you will reap what you sow according to the law of reciprocity. Which means you will be blessed if you sow good seeds with your fellow man and God, but it is a far cry from equating that with Salvation.

In fact, it is a far-reaching assumption and an erroneous one at that, since the Gospel clearly states that there is no remission of sin without the Blood of Jesus (Heb. 9:22). As Jesus said himself, in John 14:6, "I am the way and the truth and the life. No one comes to the Father except through me." Excluding all other ways/religions to heaven but directly through him, which is a very bold statement - unless it is true, just to clarify things for the believer in Christ who may be a bit confused as to what the quantum/unified field is. I submit it is where angels fear to tread, as it is where demons roam like hungry lions seeking whom they may devour. Scheming to steal the souls of men by brain washing them visa vie the intelligent spiritual atmospheric energy (SAE) of human thought and idea. They use media, Hollywood, music, social media, drugs, alcohol, pornography, counterfeit and false religion to achieve this end.

Personally, I connect with God through the Holy Spirit of Truth when I pray and meditate, as Jesus told us to in John 14:13–17: "And I will do whatever you ask in my name, so that the Father may be glorified in the Son. You may ask me for anything in my name, and I will do it. "If you love me, keep my commands (Commandments). And I will ask the Father, and he will give you another advocate to help you and be with you forever—- (even) the Spirit of truth. The world cannot accept him, because it neither sees him nor knows him. But you know him, for he lives with you and will be in you."

As you can see, even Jesus taught that good things are supposed to happen to you."

## Chapter 18

# *Revisiting Paradigms*

*Choose to believe good about yourself and life in general, because that will be the very thing you realize and materialize.*

Earlier we learned briefly about paradigms. I would like to elaborate a bit more on the topic. I want to draw a comparison between children born into wealthy families and kids born into families of scarcity. Is it any wonder that kids with parents who pinch pennies grow up to pinch pennies? The answer is no, it isn't.

The reason for this is that their paradigm is of a scarcity mindset. They always fear not having enough, so more than likely the most they will ever have is just enough. Now, contrast that with a kid born to wealthy parents. That kid will grow up with confidence about money. He will learn how to make it and nine out of ten times he will make even more of it than most people.

The difference between the two kids comes down to this: Paradigm. The paradigm of the poor kid was to fear never having enough, because it's all he ever saw at home with his mom and/or dad. He grows up not being very generous in a lot of cases, never learns how to think and use his mind to his own advantage. Never learns how to make money and manage it wisely. If it's that he's not very generous due to coming from lack, then how can he reap a bountiful harvest when he has only planted minimal seeds? Even if you don't have much, then what little you do give is generous.

It is the reason a lot of welfare recipients are fourth and fifth generation, except for those who learn how to change and break free from that cycle for a better life. They learn how to change their paradigm from a scarcity mindset to a wealthy one.

The rich kid on the other hand in a lot of cases has learned to plant by seeing his parents give and give to those who lack, witnessing the continuous harvest they receive as a result. He has a prosperous abundant mindset. See, what we are raised to believe becomes engrained in our psyche and shapes our paradigm from youth.

What most fail to realize is that they can change it. Jesus said, "According to your faith let it be done unto you" Matt 9:29. Choose to believe something new, good and different than what the world believes and teaches about wealth. Then you will be wealthy in spirit and eventually in your bank account as you move toward your goal. Proverbs 23:7 says "As a man thinketh in his heart, so is he" (KJV). The NIV Bible says, "for he is the kind of person who is always thinking about the cost." You will ultimately become what you consistently and passionately think about and therefore believe, so as, to obey.

Therefore, choose to believe good about yourself and life in general, because that will be the very thing you realize and materialize. Do you see a hostile world looking out from behind your eyes or do you see a friendly one? Your experience in how you see life treating you should answer that question for you. See, if you see a hostile world, chances are you're focused on hostility and that's all you'll ever experience for the most part, because you live your life on the defensive and purposely closed off from most people.

If you see a friendly world, then you'll find friendliness for the most part, because you're choosing to focus on the best in others and not the worst, thereby making you an inviting personality. Remember the platitude, "what you focus on you find?" You always get more of what you choose to see in the world. More of what you're looking for. All you need to do is go out and look for it—it's there. Life tends to mirror back to you what you put before it—your vibrational energy signature.

As Dr. Joe Dispenza says, "Define yourself by a vision of the future instead of your memories of the past." What a quote that is. People who dwell on their negative past are living in a victim state and when you're dwelling on the past, you're completely missing the present. Jesus said, in Matthew 6:34, "Therefore do not worry about tomorrow, for tomorrow will worry about itself. Each day has enough trouble of its own."

Same thing goes for the past. A farmer can't yield a crop from seeds he planted before the last harvest. He already harvested that crop. It's time to plant for the next harvest and planting is done in the present, right now. The "now harvest" you're experiencing in the present is a result of the seeds you planted in the past. Want a better "now harvest" in the future? Plant better seeds today.

The past is gone and can't be changed. Look around you, notice the beauty of creation and know that you can't be part of a different beautiful future unless you're a part of the creative now. You are not a victim unless you choose to be; but make no mistake about it, you'll only be a victim to the seeds of your own thoughts and remember, every seed you plant has a harvest. That harvest will come for certain.

Plant liberally the good thought/action seeds of life today on faith that according to the law of giving and receiving/sowing and reaping, you can look forward to a bountiful harvest tomorrow. Look around you at all the victims of the world who blame everyone but themselves instead of laying aside all excuses and finding a way to succeed.

The moment you decide to do this, you'll go from victim to victory. It won't happen overnight, but with consistency and a passionate belief that it can happen, you will see change in no time and the first thing that will change is your attitude toward life, then good things will begin to happen to you and for you. It's the difference between you understanding that life is happening for your betterment and not to your detriment.

Try it, but be consistent with your new positive mindset, and before I end, I would be remiss if I did not give you the opportunity to hear the simple Gospel of the Lord Jesus Christ, so you can at least make a fully informed choice to either accept His sacrifice for the eternal penalty and punishment of your sins (Rom. 6:23) or try to do it "My Way" like Frank Sinatra.

## Chapter 19

# *The Dunamis of God*

---

*The Dynamite of God unto Salvation
is the Gospel of Jesus Christ.*

The Gospel of the Lord Jesus Christ is simply this: Man is the sinner; Jesus is the Savior. God created man and man disobeyed God bringing the curse of sin upon mankind and planet earth. God had a backup plan since before the foundation of the world to send His one and only begotten Son, Jesus, to earth as a baby to be the Great Reconciler and redeemer. The Christ Messiah of Israel; Emmanuel (God with us) and all who would believe in His eternal sacrifice, repent of their sins and be baptized, born again (the spiritual re-birth) would be saved (Mk 16:16). Repentance is a complete change of mind that leads to a complete change of heart that manifests itself in a complete change of life and lifestyle.

Jesus shed His innocent blood at Calvary's cross so that mankind could be reconciled back unto God the Father once more. Jesus was Holy and wholly without sin, as He was not conceived in sin but of a virgin by the Holy Spirit. One of the main reasons God became a man was so that man would never be able to accuse Him of not knowing what it is like to be human. To suffer the way man suffers on earth and boy did Jesus ever suffer. God owes man nothing and man owes Jesus everything, because only Jesus can lay claim to this—God becoming a man to redeem mankind.

The Apostle Paul says, in Romans 1:16, "For I am not ashamed of the gospel, because it is the power of God that brings salvation to everyone who believes: first to the Jew, then to the Gentile (All Non-Jews)." The word *power* is from the Greek word *Dunamis*. It literally means "dynamite" in English. The dynamite of God unto salvation is the Gospel of Jesus Christ. It is that powerful in transforming a person's life and soul.

In Acts 2:38, Peter replied, "Repent and be baptized, every one of you, in the name of Jesus Christ for the forgiveness of your sins. And (then) you will receive the gift of the Holy Spirit" (in that order).

According to this verse, if a person offers a sincere confession of faith in Jesus Christ as personal Lord and Savior and repents of their sins, then that person's outward act of receiving baptism as the precondition of faith entitles him or her to receive the inward dwelling and spiritual illumination of the Holy Spirit of God. That person becomes born a second time into this life (and now life eternal), only this time as the spiritual birth or rebirth. Hence, this is the becoming of born again, according to the commandment of the Lord Jesus Christ in Matthew 28:19, Mark 16:16, and John 3:3–7, to walk in the newness of life, now possessing the power to obey the commandments of God.

Jesus said in, John 14:15, "If you love me, keep my commands" ("Commandments" – KJV). That does not mean keep them perfectly. It means to have a heart that longs and tries to obey. If we fail, we have an advocate with the Father in Christ Jesus (1 John 2:1). 1 John 1:9 says, "If we confess our sins, he is faithful and just and will forgive us our sins and purify us from all unrighteousness" (moral sin). This Scripture is in the continuous context.

According to the Holy Bible, that is the Gospel truth about Jesus Christ, but Jesus never forced anyone to follow him. Instead He said, "Whoever wants to be (KJV says "Will be") my disciple must deny themselves and take up their cross and follow me." (Matt. 16:24). The word *Will* being the operative word in that text, shows us Jesus appealing to the free will of a person.

However, He goes on to show the contrasting results of deciding to follow or not follow Him. Man has a choice with God always, but choices have consequences. The choice is freely and always yours to make.

Either way, if you utilize the universal principles described in this book, then good things will happen to you for the most part. From my personal experience—and believe me, I went down a tough road in my younger years, all my own making—I know whereof I speak. However, I'm still a work in progress. I turned my life around by coming to Christ and learning how to think, using the mind He gave me so that good things can happen to me. I must die to myself every day and that has been my biggest struggle, but I never quit, because Christ said He would never leave me nor forsake me (Mt 28:20; Heb 13:5).

You can too. Remember, if one man can do it another man can do it. God bless you, and Jesus loves you.

## Chapter 20

## *Never Stop Asking What If*

---

*When you ask "What If" questions, your subconscious mind automatically begins scanning your brain for every bit of information you've ever learned about anything and everything related to your "What If" question.*

When we ask questions, we gain knowledge. When we gain knowledge, we grow. When we grow, we become a different person than we were a few minutes ago before we gained that new knowledge, which altered our perception on life.

When we ask the "what if" questions, we ignite the reasoning part of our brain called the frontal lobe, which is the creative center of the brain where we feel happiness. You've heard the saying "happiness is an inside job?" Well that's true. Happiness is a state of mind, not something that happens to you to cause it. Circumstances can enhance your happiness, not cause it. Your decision to think happy thoughts which create happy feelings is all on you. Your thinking causes either happiness or sadness. Now, circumstances can stimulate you to think sad thoughts and that is normal, ergo if someone we love dies, naturally we will grieve. That's part of life and although technically we have complete control over our thoughts, outside circumstances beyond our control can sometimes overwhelm us. The key is to go through your grieving period and then allow for healing by thinking on the good memories of the person you lost and not dwelling on the fact that they're never coming back. Remember, every day you live you are moving one day closer to reuniting with them.

I have had people die on me and still chose to be happy. Was I sad for a period while grieving? Of course, but my state was one of happiness, nonetheless. I lost my older sister, Sharon, and older brother, Tommy, both to suicide eleven years apart. Then a year after Tommy died, I lost my best friend in the universe—my dad—in 2006 and then my mom in February of 2019. All four were great losses. I cried for three months after losing dad, but I was still a happy person by choice. It just took my heart a few months to heal from the freshness of such a great loss. I cried for two months when mom died, but she was older, very ill and ready to be reunited with dad, Jesus and the

# Never Stop Asking What If

rest of her family. Therefore, I grieved differently and healed more happily knowing that, but that was a very tough grieving process as well. Losing your mom is a different kind of pain than losing your dad. Those of you who have lost both understand what I mean by that.

I asked the question, what if dad had lived longer? Would I have been happy watching him suffer with his health problems the way he did for so long, just so I could converse with him and show him I loved him every day? The answer is rather obvious. He was tired of suffering and although he was willing to stay here to make mom happy, feel her love and the love of his children, he was just ready to go home to be with the Lord and the rest of his family.

I was ok with that, because I understood from a biblical perspective that if I could peek behind the veil into Heaven and see the peace dad now has with Jesus—no pain, no tears, only joy unspeakable—I'd say, "dad, you stay here and enjoy the eternal peace you longed for your whole life on earth." I comforted my mother with that thought to help her cope with his loss after building a life with him for fifty-two years. She survived more than twelve years since then without him because of the love her family gave her and because of her good family genes.

I asked, what if Sharon and Tommy had lived? I imagined both in perfect mental health, living happy, peaceful lives with their spouses and children. But that would have been extremely hard for them because of their addictions. They were in such mental and, therefore emotional anguish they just felt that dying would be much easier for them. I can only pray that God's un-coveted mercies are extended to mentally suffering souls like that. I need to believe they are.

Those kinds of "what if" questions are different than the ones I'm referring to in this chapter. I'm talking about asking, "What if I could be among the best entertainers in the world?" Or, "What if I could be one of the best inspirational Author/Speakers in the world?"

When you ask "what if" questions in that context, your subconscious mind automatically begins scanning your brain for every bit of information you have ever learned about anything and everything related to your "what if" question. Then it will match you with it to the best of its ability, according to the information it has been given regarding.

"Please write down five "what if" questions right now. Be creative. Think about those possibilities. Spend some quality time every morning and every evening dreaming, envisioning, visualizing, believing that you will accomplish, achieve and manifest these positive thoughts and ideas."

Therefore, it is imperative that you read up on all the knowledge regarding these questions that you can find. Once it is in your brain, your subconscious mind can put it all together and come up with an ingenious idea or ideas to help you make that "what if" a reality.

When you're seeking a creative idea or answer to something, the human mind takes all the information you've taken in through the eyes and ears to create that idea and give you that answer. Therefore, read and listen to as much of the right information as you can, so your mind has enough to draw on in its creative process.

EPILOGUE

# *The Last Word*

---

*I* was watching the Green Bay/Dallas playoff game. My Fiancée is a huge Cowboys fan - Boooo! (Laughing), so I had no choice (I'm a New England Patriots fan). She always wanted to be a Dallas Cowboys Cheerleader since she was a little girl. I received a phone call from my older brother, Brian. We got to talking about how I was finishing up writing this book you're now reading. He reminded me that in the early days of our parents, America was great because most people believed in God, went to Church, and songs on the radio were indicative of a moral society—songs with positive lyrics of believing in the American dream. The message that you could be anything you wanted to be because you lived in the most affluent country the world has ever known. Songs like "Get Happy," "Swinging on a Star,"

"Pick Yourself Up," and "High Hopes" are just a few of those songs and among some of my all-time favorites.

Brian's point was if you could conceive it and believe it, then you could achieve it and receive it. Most people back in the 1950s understood this concept. Unlike today, where more people than ever before believe they're cursed and that bad things are supposed to happen to them. It's completely understandable as it's all they ever see on the news and thus it is programmed into their subconscious minds, turning them into zombie robots.

It's very sad that television has programmed Americans to live in fear and give up on their creative dreams, in favor of just living an average cookie cutter life. Whatever happened to the public service announcements (PSAs) that used to air on television in the 70s and 80s? Whose call was it to stop those ads? The dumbing down of the American society has reached an all-time high in 2019, and I'm not going to sit on the sidelines when I can do something about it. I'll write as many books as I need to in order to reach as many readers as I can to inspire them to be the best individual version of themselves that they can be in this life.

People who seek trouble without fail will always find it. People who seek goodness and kindness without fail will always find it.

Jesus Christ said, "Ask and it shall be given you; Seek and ye shall find; Knock and it shall be open unto you."

You will achieve what you intend and seek out in this life but in its own time, and just because you may encounter a few storms, it does not mean you're not headed into the sun light God plans to shine upon you. Your path and your destination are not to be confused. Good things are supposed to happen to you and *for* you, but if you are not mentally open to receive your good, you will not receive it. It's that simple.

Earl Nightingale said, "We become what we think about most of the time, and that's the strangest secret."

He's right, not because it sounds right, but because history proves it. If you do not give up on your dream/goal no matter how long it takes, you will achieve it to one degree or another, but you will achieve. The key is to find out what you love and think on that. Obsess over it every day until it begins to develop in your life and see it through to completion. You've got to hold onto your vision and keep moving toward it until it manifests.

Say your affirmations every day after your prayers, and then believe your prayers and affirmations. Soon enough they will develop in your life as you move one foot in front of the other toward your goals.

Some people say to me, "But, Joey, you repeat your affirmations over and over. Isn't that what the Bible calls vain repetition?" They're referring to Matthew 6:7–8, where Jesus says "And when you pray, do not keep on babbling ("Vain Repetition" – KJV) like pagans, for they think they will be heard because of their many words. Do not be like them, for your Father knows what you need before you ask him."

My answer to that is my prayers are different than my affirmations. I pray to the Father in the name of Jesus like I'm talking to my own father. It's a conversation, and it's positive. I thank Him for my current blessings and my future blessings. I don't repeat prayers like a robot or like I'm repeating an incantation. When I say my daily affirmations, it's for the purpose of reprogramming my subconscious mind to eventually yield me the positive things I plant there.

My pastor always says, "Whatever you tell your subconscious mind is what it will spit back at you, like a computer finishes the words you type before you finish typing them, as it remembers what you typed into its hard drive the very first time."

We have the ability to teach the subconscious mind to think like a winner by placing winning commands there, like, "I am healthy, wealthy and wise. I am holy, sober and temperate. I am a magnate for money and love. I have a lavish steady dependable income, consistent with integrity and mutual benefit." These are just a few examples of daily positive affirmations that I have learned through research and that you can also use to reprogram your subconscious mind. You don't even have to believe them at first. Just continuously say them daily until your subconscious mind is reprogrammed, and you do believe them.

Once reprogrammed, the subconscious mind has to find a way to make you a winner, much like the person who self-deprecates becomes the very negative things they train their subconscious mind to believe—that they are a loser in life, which is a lie, unless they continue to give life to that belief by feeding those negative thoughts with more thoughts like them.

Once you make a definiteness of purpose for your life and decide to move in that direction, the laws of the universe as God created them will begin to bring about that reality. Something must happen because you set that spiritual atmospheric energy (SAE) into motion with your belief that you will be successful no matter what.

This is the reason it is so vitally important to consult God before defining your own life purpose. For it may not be in line with His purpose for your life and ultimately although He will try to guide you onto His path, if you choose your own way first it may be detrimental to you. There may also likely be unnecessary heartache, bumps and bruises along with uncomfortable readjustments to get you either onto or back onto the right pathway for your life.

So long as you are alive you have the personal power to change your life by changing your thought patterns. If you think you are a loser or a failure, it's because you choose to live like that and will remain a victim to that line of thinking until you decide to change it. Again, the good news is, so long as you are alive and breathing, *you* (and only you) can change it, and you can begin to change it right now.

The choice is yours but make no bones about it, man becomes what he consistently thinks about, so be careful and mindful to be your own best friend and not your own worst enemy. "Do not conform to the pattern of this world; but be transformed by the renewing of your mind. Then you will be able to test and approve what God's will is— his good, pleasing and perfect will." (Rom.12:2).

## THE SUPPLEMENT

# *Seven Steps to Achieve any Goal*

---

1. Pray about what you want - God knows what you want more than you do. Ask Him and He will show you. It may take a little while, but in His time, I promise He will show you. More often if He makes you wait, He's just trying to develop you as a person and to see how bad you really want what you're asking for. If you keep on asking and moving toward it, it shows Him that you want it more than anything else.

Whatever you do, don't be wishy washy. You need to know what you want if you're ever going to get it. The Apostle Paul said, in Philippians 4:6, "Do not be anxious about anything, but in every situation, by prayer and petition, with thanksgiving, present your requests to God."

Remember, God made the vehicle and the engine inside the vehicle. Your mind is the engine and proper education allows you to utilize more of your thinking mind. The human mind is the greatest machine God ever created. Learn how to use it. Ask Him to specifically and definitively show you. He will!

2. Meditate on it - Meditation centers, balance and prepares you to give and receive all good things. It regulates your blood pressure, helps you to focus on peace of mind and soul, and most importantly, it's where your most effective visioneering is done.
3. Visualize it vividly - We create things twice, first in the mind, then in the body. Envision your goal in detail. See it through to the end in your mind first and then it will ultimately happen in the body. Always see the end-result in your mind of you achieving it and only focus on that.

Remember, focus concentration or visioneering is a skill based on neuroscience principles.

Your subconscious mind creates a habitual memory loop that reinforces your goal commands and goes to work to help you manifest it into the tangible from the intangible.

## SEVEN STEPS TO ACHIEVE ANY GOAL

4. Set your intention - Intend to follow through with your specific goal once you've set it in motion by doing at least one thing every day toward that goal until it comes to pass - again, no matter how long it takes.

Intention is the most powerful thing because you are shifting the gear from park to drive, ready to punch the gas and accelerate forward motion. With intention there's no buyer's remorse. You either intend to do it or you don't. Be decisive, know exactly what you want and always remember, life responds favorably to the bold.

5. Use positive affirmations - Daily positive affirmations reprogram your subconscious mind. The more you give the same command over and over to your subconscious mind, the more you are retraining it to eventually believe it automatically without you having to consciously give the command. That is your autonomic system.
6. Take cogent action - Positive, deliberate, consistent daily action creates a magnetic gravitational energy vortex that pulls what you need toward you to help facilitate your goals. You're the one who releases the energy it takes. You generate it with your thoughts, which give birth to your feelings. But then you need to follow through with

the intelligent, convincing action that focuses the power of that energy like a laser beam. The word *action* is part of the word *satisfaction*. Desire for satisfaction leads to dynamic action, and therein lies fulfillment and success.

Read and listen to everything there is to learn about your goal so your subconscious mind can use that information to give you the most creative ideas in order to make that goal a manifest reality.

Though it won't be easy (otherwise everyone would do it) and more than likely won't happen right away, don't quit—*ever*. Ninety-nine percent of all failures are the result of people quitting too soon.

That extra mile is never crowded, so don't ever stop moving toward your goal. After all, the time is going to pass anyway. Stick-to-it-iveness is key in achieving your goals. If you were starving and there was a line to get food, no matter how long that line was you'd stand in it. Even if it was twenty miles long and you couldn't see the tent up ahead with the food being served, you'd stand in it because of the promise that you'd be fed. Besides, fact is the time is going to pass anyway, so stick to your goal and stay in line. Eventually, inch by slow grinding inch, you'll get to the front and it will be your turn to be fed. All that waiting will have been worth it.

## Seven Steps To Achieve Any Goal

7. Give back and express gratitude - If you want more blessings in your life, you must give a tithe of your first fruits (10% before taxes), either to your local church or to those less fortunate, or both. Also, give an offering. You can never out-give God (Read Malachi 3 regarding Tithes & Offerings).

If you don't belong to a church, I recommend you find one. There's nothing more fulfilling than a loving church family that you'll be headed to eternity with when Christ returns or he takes you home, whichever comes first. Nevertheless, you could give an offering to those in the community who are in need or to a charity that is near and dear to your heart.

You need to plant seeds by giving back or you will not have much of a harvest to reap. You have a great big fertile field of soil called "Humanity" to sow plenty of seeds in. Remember, you can't out give God and his law of sowing and reaping. It's a *law*—like gravity. It's called the law of reciprocity or the law of giving and receiving, and remember, we reap what we sow, more than we sow, later than we sow.

Giving is seed planting and you can't reap a goal harvest unless you plant charity seeds, which brings me to gratitude. You need to be a grateful soul in order to give with a cheerful heart. The Apostle Paul said, in 2 Corinthians 9:7, "Each of you should give what you have decided in your heart to give, not reluctantly or under compulsion, for God loves a cheerful giver."

If you are ungrateful, you will never part with your money for others in need, because in your own mind nobody is in more need than you are and even if/when you do give, your motive will be all wrong. It's the difference between either being dragged to a work party or showing up early before anyone arrives to help decorate the room.

Be a grateful giver. Gratitude for what you have (a lot or a little) ensures that you'll give to those in need out of love and empathy in spirit. Therefore, you will always have more to give and be grateful for because charity and gratitude go hand in hand.

Also—and this is the key to bringing more into your life to be grateful for—learn to be grateful in advance for your ideals as if you have already received them. You just need to believe beyond any shadow of a doubt that you will achieve them. Doubt says, "I'll believe it when I see it." Faith says, "I'll see it when I believe it." Therefore, exercise great faith.

This is how you will feel the advanced gratitude I speak of that will bring it to pass in your life. Jesus taught us this principle in Mark 11:24: "Therefore I tell you, whatever you ask for in prayer, believe that you have (already) received it, and it will be yours." That, my friends, is a lesson in visioneering from the Lord Jesus Christ. I call it "advanced gratitude." Humble gratitude is the most magnetic force in the universe, because it is shown with the motive of love.

I want to end with this statement about the difference between hope and faith. Biblical hope was supposed to mean something we look forward to with great faith like the second coming of Jesus on the last day of Earth's history. However, the word *hope* in today's world means "maybe it will happen; maybe it won't?" That's not faith at all. So please remember this saying: Hope tip toes through the fire just hoping to not get burned. Faith leaps over it. Jesus left absolutely no room for doubt in Mark 11:24 when we pray for something.

Jesus loves you, and may God always shine his rich blessings upon you.

If you enjoyed reading this book, I encourage you to check back at www.JoeyNoone.com or www.JoeyVoices.com for more to come. Thank you for reading, and remember, that extra mile is never crowded!

***All Scripture is from NIV**

# *Acknowledgements*

Colleen (My Fiancée), Cadence and Brylie (daughters) – for their patience with my reclusiveness at times, so I could dive in and zone out in order to write my books! I know I do it at the most inconvenient times, but you never know when inspiration to write or ideas about what is already in progress will hit you and it just cannot wait when it hits, or it will be lost. I can't imagine how that feels to have your significant other and man of the home distance himself from you at times. I do apologize for it, but it is a necessary process for a writer. I will however do all I can to make up for it! I love you All! Thank You for your support and Colleen, for your sound advice when I need it in my writing! It is truly invaluable!

Bob Hyldburg (Author of Total Patriots Encyclopedia) – for his co-editing contributions to this book! I have learned a lot about the process of writing and editing from him. Thank You Bob!

---

Paul Solano – for inspiring me to write my first book after many weekly discussions about my life philosophy. He saw talent in me to teach, write and I'm grateful for having him as my good friend in helping me find that within myself. Thank You for that Paul, and for doing the initial book formatting, as I had no idea how to do it. You're a good friend!

---

My Fans – for their undying support and belief in me! Even when I went through my midlife crisis. Also, for pre-ordering this book! It helped to pay it off for a quicker book release. Thank You!

---

Foreword and Reviewers – for taking the time to pre-read this book and giving me your heart felt, honest thoughts on it. I am forever grateful to you all for your kindness toward me! Thank You!

# *Reviews*

From first page to last, Joey helps to deliver a book on how God can use time to divinely move in our lives. This book is an in-depth read expressing how we humans are so much more than the physical bodies we walk around in, and how we should be more aware of the world around us regarding the realms of negative and positive thinking.

Joey has poured in knowledge that he has learned throughout his journey, along with colorful detailed personal experiences. He ties in God throughout, and how our faith plays a vital role in making great things happen. We have "sixteen hours to inspire, motivate, or teach at least one person. Sixteen hours to make a difference in someone's life including your own." Thank you for the priceless reminder, Joey!

—Jennifer Ross
HuffPost blogger, and author of *Isaiah's Story*

Reading Joey Noone's book, *Good Things are Supposed to Happen to YOU* was spiritual, positive and very uplifting. Joey brings his extensive knowledge of the Bibles teaching's from more than two centuries ago into today's world. Understanding that life is what we see, feel and how we react to it. It is God's gift to all of us. Joey writes using quotes and gives examples on how to live a full rich life.

—Charley Valera
Author of the award-winning book, *My Father's War: Memories from Our Honored WWII Soldiers*

I found Joey Noone's book, *Good Things Are Supposed to Happen to YOU*, to be amazingly true! What an incredibly interesting read! It made me wonder why certain things over the years had happened to me and as I read on, it all began to make sense to me. Joey breaks it down so well to the understanding mind. This book is no doubt God implied.

After reading it, a good friend of mine out in Texas popped into my mind out of the blue. About an hour later he called me after nine months of no correspondence whatsoever! I told him how his name came to mind that morning and then he called me shortly thereafter. I explained how that type of thing happens scientifically after reading about it in Joey's book.

I also called my other good friend and Former National League Cy Young Award winner Steve Bedrosian after reading this book and reminded him of how we would mentally visualize for example a curve ball breaking over the plate in just the right way and how that mental picture helped to throw it correctly.

In Pro Baseball I've learned that 'Vivid Visualization' is a must have in order to succeed! Don't miss this read! You will be enlightened for sure and I have no doubt it will be a huge success! Congrats Joey Noone my good friend! Keep inspiring!

—Dave Caiazzo
Former pitcher, longtime major league baseball scout (Indians, Angels), and author of
*Life Tried to Throw Me a Curveball*

Every word of Joey Voices's *Good Things Are Supposed to Happen to YOU* is pure inspiration.

Joey's stories of hope, happiness, and guidance are told in a readable, honest prose style that will continue to inspire long after the last amazing page is turned. Good Things is a brilliant guiding light indeed!

—Andrew McAleer
Adjunct Professor, Boston College, and author of
*Positive Results*

*Joey Noone © 2019 All Rights Reserved*

CPSIA information can be obtained
at www.ICGtesting.com
Printed in the USA
FFHW011720050919
54792522-60469FF